Chart II

ga	が	gi	ぎ	gu	ぐ	ge	げ	go	ご
za	ざ	ji	じ	zu	ず	ze	ぜ	zo	ぞ
da	だ	ji	ぢ	zu	づ	de	で	do	ど
ba	ば	bi	び	bu	ぶ	be	べ	bo	ぼ
pa	ぱ	pi	ぴ	pu	ぷ	pe	ぺ	po	ぽ

Chart III

kya	きゃ	kyu	きゅ	kyo	きょ
sha	しゃ	shu	しゅ	sho	しょ
cha	ちゃ	chu	ちゅ	cho	ちょ
nya	にゃ	nyu	にゅ	nyo	にょ
hya	ひゃ	hyu	ひゅ	hyo	ひょ
mya	みゃ	myu	みゅ	myo	みょ
rya	りゃ	ryu	りゅ	ryo	りょ

gya	ぎゃ	gyu	ぎゅ	gyo	ぎょ
ja	じゃ	ju	じゅ	jo	じょ

bya	びゃ	byu	びゅ	byo	びょ
pya	ぴゃ	pyu	ぴゅ	pyo	ぴょ

（財）海外技術者研修協会 編著

Self-Study Kana Workbook

Learning through Listening and Writing

英語版

一人(ひとり)で学(まな)べる

ひらがな かたかな

スリーエーネットワーク

Published by 3A Corporation.
Trusty Kojimachi Bldg., 2F, 4, Kojimachi 3-Chome, Chiyoda-ku, Tokyo 102-0083, Japan

ISBN978-4-88319-158-1 C0081

First published 2000
Printed in Japan

Five features of this book

1. Step learning method that enables you to study smoothly

This book is designed to enable you to advance smoothly in three steps or stages - from listening, to reading and finally writing - ensuring you gain a thorough grounding in what you are learning. Each lesson consists of three pages on average, permitting you to pace your daily study easily.

2. Maximum use of the CD

The listening and reading practices in all the lessons require you to use the CD, allowing you to not only learn the kana letters but also to acquire the standard pronunciation and accent of the Japanese language.

3. Handwritten model letters

The shapes of printed letters are somewhat different from the shapes of handwritten ones, due to the design incorporated into printing type. We have employed handwritten letters as our model for the writing practice of each letter, because they are more simple and natural. Examples of common mistakes made by beginners are shown in the example boxes entitled "Wrong". They will help prevent you from memorizing the shapes of letters incorrectly.

4. Emphasis on practical words

This book allows you to concentrate on learning simple and practical words, which are mainly selected from basic level Japanese language textbooks. In particular, the **Listening and Writing Exercise** and **Test** sections, which conclude your study, include carefully selected words frequently used in daily life. As the objective is to improve your ability to write kana letters, rely on the Roman writing system as little as possible. For the same reason, the translation of these sections, sentences written in the Roman writing system and answers to questions are compiled separately at the back of the book.

5. Various exercises

The **Summary Practice** sections enable you to check your level of understanding and to review what you have learned, and incorporate quizzes and puzzles so as to maintain your interest in learning the letters and to prevent you from becoming bored. You can effectively make progress in learning by yourself in a pleasurable manner. Reading the columns on Japanese letters and pronunciation will give you more interest in kana letters and Japanese language study in general.

この本の５つの特徴

１．無理なく学べるステップ学習

聞く練習から読む練習、そして書く練習へと段階を追って、無理なく学習が進められます。１課あたり平均３ページで構成され、毎日の学習ペースがつかみやすくなっています。

２．CDをフル活用

聞く練習、読む練習など、全ての課でCDを使用するようになっています。これによって、単なるかな学習にとどまらず、日本語の標準的な発音、アクセントも身に付けられます。

３．手書きのモデル文字

印刷字体はデザインされた字体であるため、手書きの文字とは微妙な違いがあります。このため、１字ずつ書く練習においては無駄がなく、より自然な手書きの文字をモデルに採用しました。

また、初心者が書き誤りやすい字形を「誤りの例」として提示しましいた。これらの例によって、誤った字形を身に付けてしまうのを防ぐことができます。

４．実用的な単語を繰り返し練習

主に、初級日本語教科書でよく使われている単語の中から選ばれた、やさしい、実用的な単語が繰り返し学習できるようになっています。特に、学習の最後の仕上げにあたる「聞いて書き取る練習」や「テスト」では、生活の中で頻繁に使われる実用的な単語を厳選しました。ローマ字にできるだけ頼らずにかなを書く実力をつけるため、これらの練習の翻訳、ローマ字表記、解答は別冊にしてあります。

５．多彩な練習問題

学習定着度がチェックでき、復習にもなる「まとめの練習」、クイズ、パズルなどを織り込んで、ともすれば単調になりがちな文字の学習を飽きずに続けられるよう工夫しました。まったく一人でも楽しく、効果的に学習を進めることができます。

練習の合間には、日本語の文字、発音などに関する「コラム」にも目を通してみてください。かな学習、日本語学習に対する興味がさらに広がることでしょう。

CONTENTS

Part II.　KATAKANA

Before You Start

In the Japanese writing system, each kana (hiragana and katakana) corresponds to a sound. Both hiragana and katakana consist of 46 letters each. The table below indicates the basic sounds of Japanese. Before you start learning the kana, listen to the accompanying CD (found at the back of the book) and familiarize yourself with these sounds.

Nihon-go no hatsuon (Pronunciation of Japanese)

Rōmaji (The Roman Alphabet)	
Hiragana	Katakana

a		i		u		e		o	
あ	ア	い	イ	う	ウ	え	エ	お	オ
ka		ki		ku		ke		ko	
か	カ	き	キ	く	ク	け	ケ	こ	コ
sa		shi		su		se		so	
さ	サ	し	シ	す	ス	せ	セ	そ	ソ
ta		chi		tsu		te		to	
た	タ	ち	チ	つ	ツ	て	テ	と	ト
na		ni		nu		ne		no	
な	ナ	に	ニ	ぬ	ヌ	ね	ネ	の	ノ
ha		hi		fu		he		ho	
は	ハ	ひ	ヒ	ふ	フ	へ	ヘ	ほ	ホ
ma		mi		mu		me		mo	
ま	マ	み	ミ	む	ム	め	メ	も	モ
ya				yu				yo	
や	ヤ			ゆ	ユ			よ	ヨ
ra		ri		ru		re		ro	
ら	ラ	り	リ	る	ル	れ	レ	ろ	ロ
wa								o	
わ	ワ							を	ヲ
n									
ん	ン								

Symbol and Numbers in Japanese

The symbol at the beginning of the practices and quizzes means that you should listen to the accompanying CD. Below the symbol are numbers indicating which part of the CD you should listen to. You are advised to learn how to read numbers in Japanese first, since the numbers on the CD are recorded in Japanese.

1	ichi	2	ni	3	san	4	yon, shi	5	go
6	roku	7	nana, shichi	8	hachi	9	kyū, ku	10	jū
11	jū ichi	12	jū ni	13	jū san	20	ni-jū		
35	san-jū go	46	yon-jū roku						
Ex.	1 - 1		ichi no ichi						

Learning Method

The practice sections of chapters [1] to [8] proceed in the following manner:

The **Listening Practice** at the beginning of each chapter is there for you to learn the shape of each letter while familiarizing yourself with its pronunciation. For those of you who find it difficult to memorize the shapes, the **Hiragana Picture Cards** at the end of this book may be helpful, allowing you to memorize each letter through the image of a picture.

With the **Summary Practice**, you can review practically what you have learnt with the CD in the following way:

Reading → Listening and Writing Exercise

As the flow of the practices is different in some later chapters, the following symbols are used to indicate how the practices should be done in this book.

Symbol	Type of Practice	Practice Method
	Listening	Memorize the shape of the letters while listening to the CD.
	Reading	Listen to the CD and repeat.
	Reading	Read aloud the letters, and listen to the CD to check if your reading is correct.
	Writing	Write the letters carefully, paying due attention to their shape.
	Listening and Writing Exercise	Write the words while listening to the CD.
	Quiz, Test	Write the answers, following the instructions.
	Quiz, Test	Write the answers while listening to the CD.

* Translations and answers to the Listening and Writing Exercises, Quizzes, and Tests are compiled at the back of the book.

Column 1 Japanese Script

Three kinds of letters are used in Japanese: hiragana and katakana, which phonetically represent the sounds of Japanese, and kanji, which represent meaning. Hiragana and katakana consist of 46 letters each, while about 2,000 kanji are used in daily life.

One of the features of the Japanese writing system is that these three kinds of letters are used in combination to write a sentence.

Example: レストランで 家族と 食事します。
○ ◆ △ ◆ △ ◆

(Resutoran de kazoku to shokuji-shimasu.)

((I) have dinner with my family at a restaurant.)

◆ Hiragana
○ Katakana
△ Kanji

For the convenience of foreigners, the Roman alphabet (Rōmaji)is sometimes used for station names, on signboards, etc.

In this textbook, you will first learn hiragana and then katakana. (For the differences between hiragana and katakana, please see page 59.)

PART I
HIRAGANA
ひらがな

Hiragana words in the pictures

きっぷうりば	kippu-uriba (ticket office)
あぶない	abunai (dangerous)
くすり	kusuri (medicine)
とまれ	tomare (stop)
おみやげ	omiyage (souvenir)

1　あ　い　う　え　お

1. Listening Practice

Try to remember the shapes of the following letters while listening to their pronunciation.

あ　い　う　え　お

a	i	u	e	o
ka	ki	ku	ke	ko
sa	shi	su	se	so
ta	chi	tsu	te	to
na	ni	nu	ne	no
ha	hi	fu	he	ho
ma	mi	mu	me	mo
ya	(i)	yu	(e)	yo
ra	ri	ru	re	ro
wa	(i)	(u)	(e)	o
n				

2. Reading Practice

Read aloud the following letters. Then listen to the CD.

1）あ　い　う　え　お
　　え　あ　い　お　う

2）うえ　あう　あおい

3. Quiz

Find the same letter as the one in the central circle.

Example

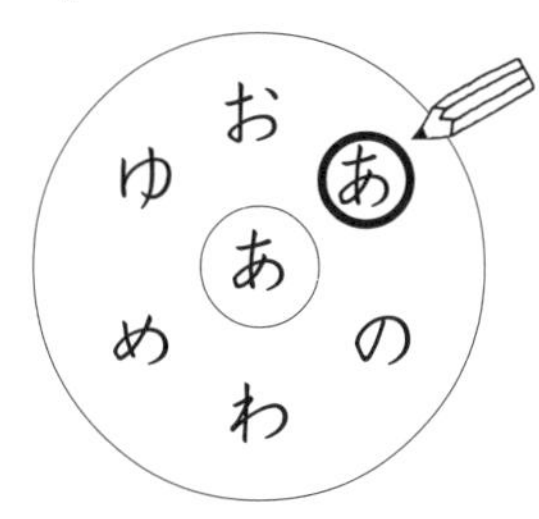

1）

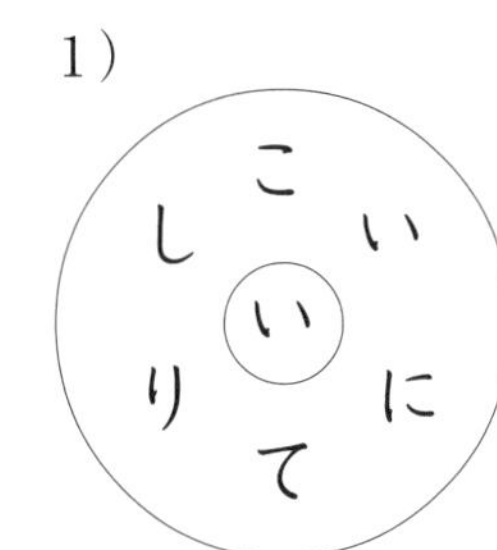

2）

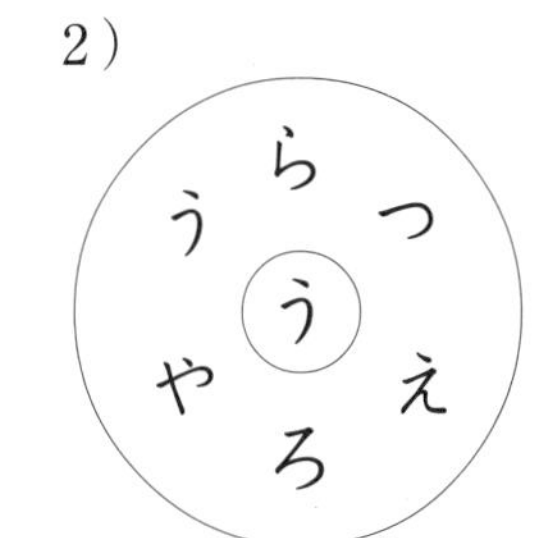

3）

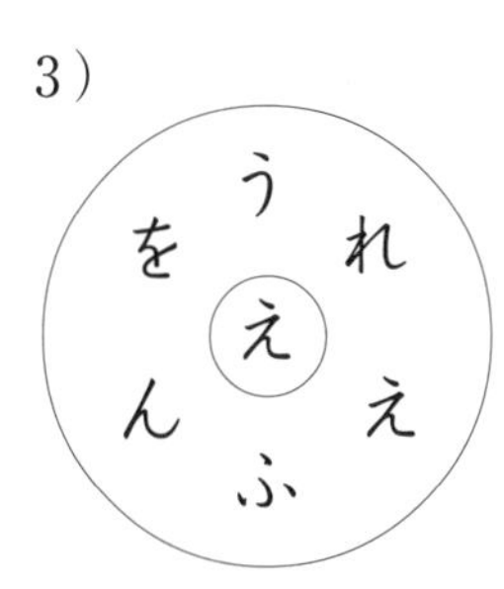

4）

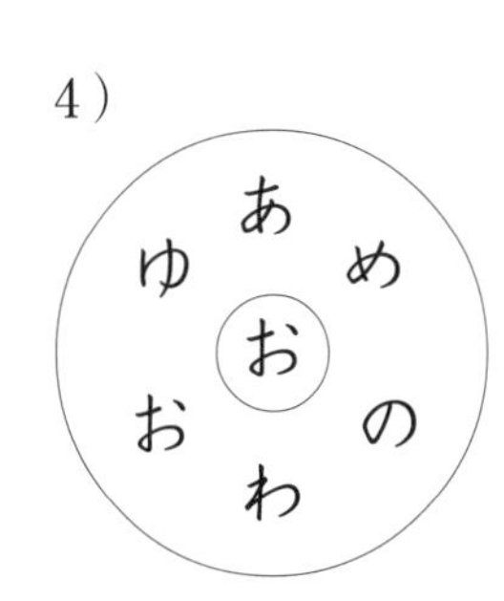

4. Writing Practice

Remember the two following points when you write hiragana.
① Follow the stroke order.
② Draw each line either from top to bottom or from left to right.

How to practice:
① In order to learn the shape of each letter, first trace the lightly written letter carefully.
② Remember the balance of the whole letter using the crossed dotted line as a guideline.

Common Mistakes

Examples of common mistakes are shown at the extreme right so that you yourself will avoid such mistakes and not write letters incorrectly.

How to read the example mistakes:
① The wrong part is circled. Compare it with the model on the extreme left. (Ex.: u う)
② When a letter is out of position or out of shape, the proper shape or line is shown in dotted lines. Thin, direct lines are guidelines for keeping the balance. (Ex.: ko こ)
③ When part of a line is longer than it should be, the correct length is shown by a thin, direct line and the mark "×". (Ex.: ke け)

Now, let's start practicing.
First, trace the lightly written letters. Then write them by yourself in the boxes.

								Wrong	
あ a	あ	あ	あ	あ		あ		あ	あ
い i	い	い	い			い		い	い
う u	う	う	う			う		う	う

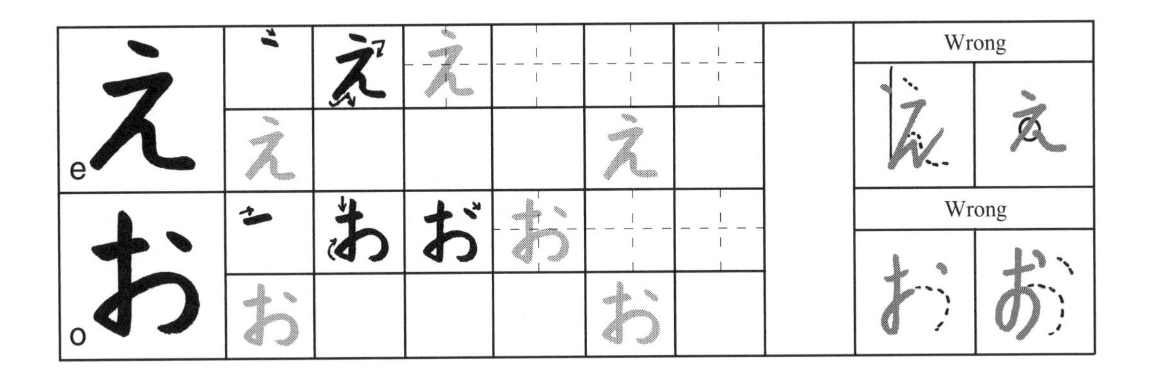

5. Let's write them once again.

First, trace the lightly written letters. Then write them by yourself.

6. Let's write some words!

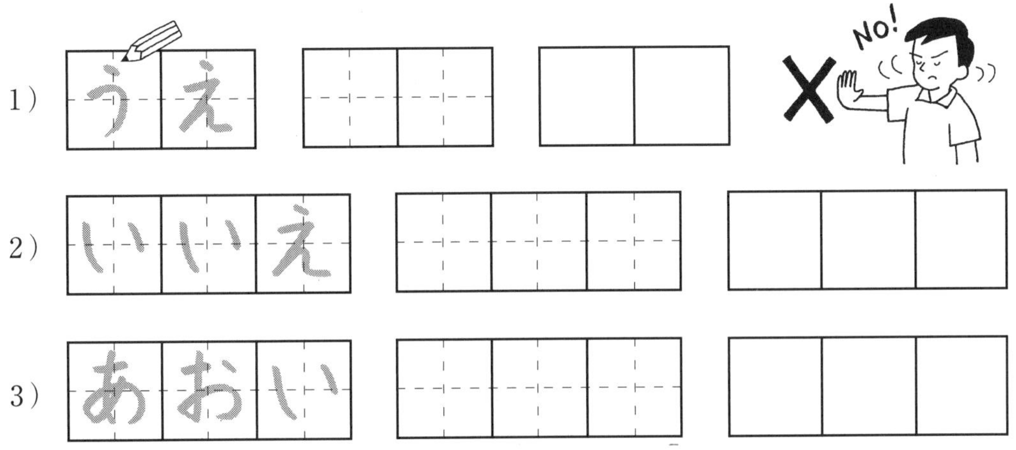

6. 1) ue (on, above)　2) iie (no)　3) aoi (blue)

2 かきくけこ、がぎぐげご

1. Listening Practice

Try to remember the shape of the following letters while listening to their pronunciation.

かきくけこ

a	i	u	e	o
ka	ki	ku	ke	ko
sa	shi	su	se	so
ta	chi	tsu	te	to
na	ni	nu	ne	no
ha	hi	fu	he	ho
ma	mi	mu	me	mo
ya	(i)	yu	(e)	yo
ra	ri	ru	re	ro
wa	(i)	(u)	(e)	o
n				

2. Reading Practice

Read aloud the following letters. Then listen to the CD.

1) か　き　く　け　こ
　 き　け　こ　か　く

2) かお　いく　こえ　きかい

3. Listening Practice

As you can hear on the CD, the pronunciation changes when the mark " ゛ " is added to か, き, く, け and こ.

がぎぐげご

ga	gi	gu	ge	go
za	ji	zu	ze	zo
da	ji	zu	de	do
ba	bi	bu	be	bo
pa	pi	pu	pe	po

4. Reading Practice

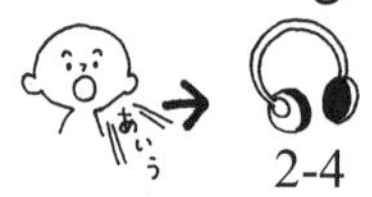

1) が　ぎ　ぐ　げ　ご
　 ぐ　げ　ぎ　が　ご

2) けが　かぎ　がいこく　ごご

5. Quiz

Connect the letters in the order of が, ぎ, ぐ, げ and ご.

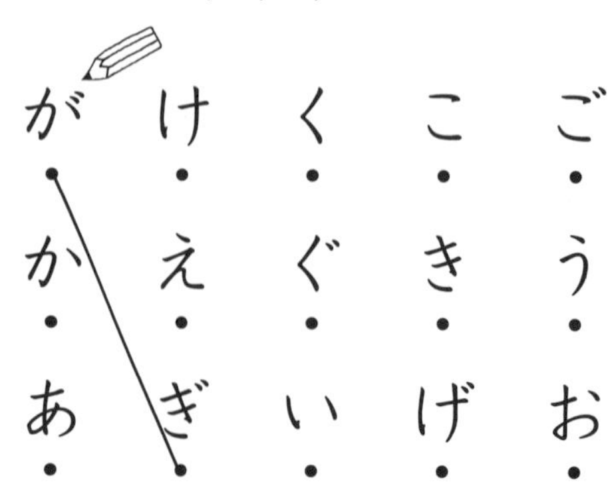

6. Writing Practice

								Wrong	
か ka	か				か			か	が
き ki	き				き			き	き
く ku	く				く			く	く
け ke	け				け			け	け
こ ko	こ				こ			こ	こ

* き can be also written as き.

As shown below, *ga*, *gi*, *gu*, *ge* and *go* are written by adding two dots to か, き, く, け and こ.

						Wrong	
が ga	が				が	が	が

ぎ gi	ぎ		ぐ gu	ぐ		
げ ge	げ		ご go	ご		

7. Let's write them once again.

First, trace the lightly written letters. Then write them by yourself.

か	き	く	け	こ
か	き	く	け	こ
か	き	く	け	こ

が	ぎ	ぐ	げ	ご
が	ぎ	ぐ	げ	ご
が	ぎ	ぐ	げ	ご

8. Let's write some words!

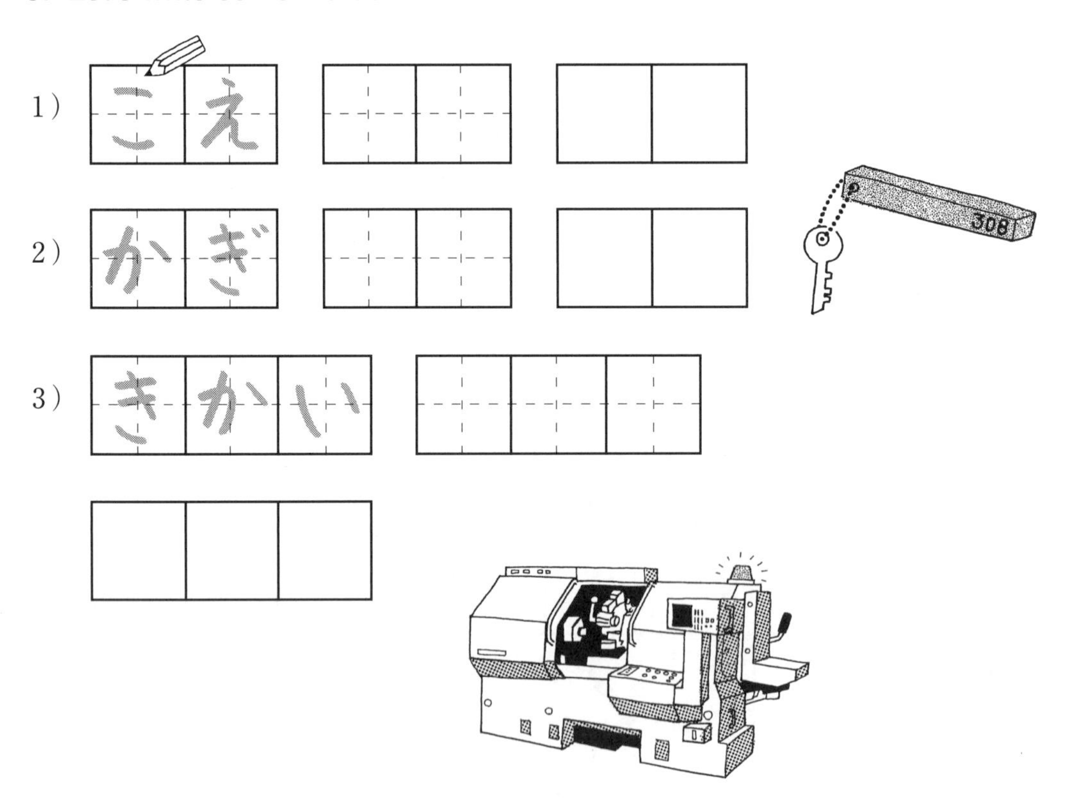

8. 1) koe (voice)　2) kagi (key)　3) kikai (machine)

Column 2　　Japanese Accent

It is said that Japanese has many homonyms, or words with the same pronunciation but different meanings. These words, however, can often be differentiated in terms of meaning by the difference in the degree of highness and lowness of the sound, i.e., the pitch accent. For example, the meanings of "はし/ hashi" can be distinguished by pronouncing "は/ ha" at a high pitch and "し / shi" at a low pitch, meaning "chopsticks", and "は/ ha" at a low pitch and "し / shi" at a high pitch, meaning "bridge."

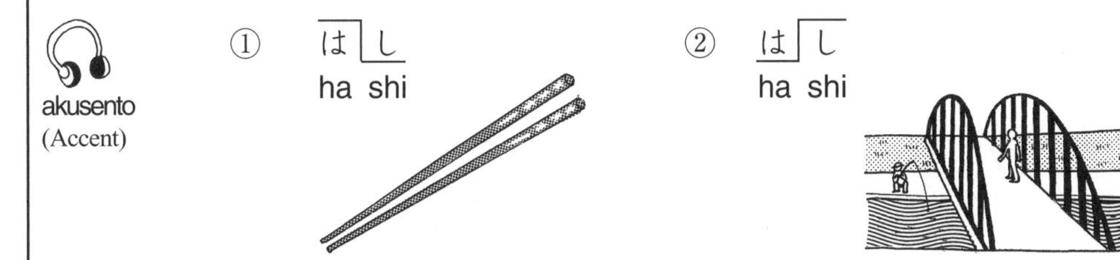

Besides indicating different meanings, the pitch accent clarifies the linkage of words as shown in the examples below.

③ まいにち　しんぶんを　よみます。　(I) read a newspaper every day.

Mainichi　shinbun o　yomimasu.

④ 『まいにちしんぶん』を　よみます。　(I) read the *Mainichi.*

There are regional differences in the accent pattern. It is especially well-known that the same words are pronounced with greatly different accent patterns in the Tokyo and Osaka areas. はし (bridge) in the example above is pronounced using a standard Japanese accent, which is based on the way of speaking in and around Tokyo. In the Osaka area, however, the accent pattern is はし, the opposite of that of standard Japanese.

Summary Practice (1 – 2)

1. Reading Practice

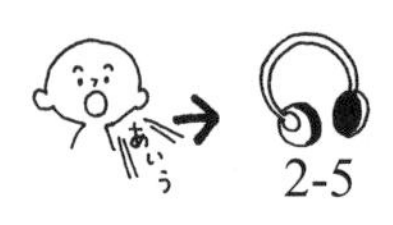

Read the following words and then listen to the CD to check the accent.

2-5

1) うえ

2) こえ

3) けが

4) かぎ

5) あおい

6) がいこく

2. Listening and Writing Exercise

Listen to the CD and write down the words in hiragana in the boxes.

2-6

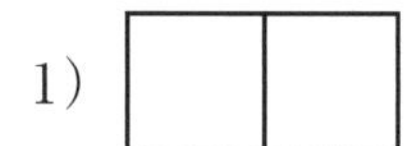

1) □□

2) □□

3) □□

4) □□

5) □□□

6) □□□

7) □□□□

NOTES　Pronunciation of *ga*, *gi*, *gu*, *ge* and *go*

Generally, when *g* is at the beginning of a word, it is pronounced hard (ex. *gaikoku*), but in other positions, it is usually pronounced as a nasal consonant (ex. *kagi*, *kega*). However, the meaning of the word is the same with either pronunciation. So, many Japanese people do not use the nasal *g* nowadays.

3 さ し す せ そ、ざ じ ず ぜ ぞ

1. Listening Practice

3-1 さ　し　す　せ　そ

2. Reading Practice

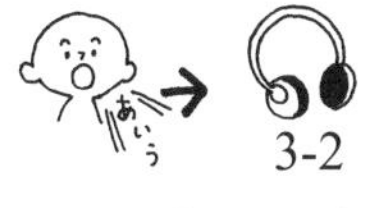
3-2

1） さ　し　す　せ　そ
　　さ　し　せ　そ　す

2） かさ　しお　うそ　すこし　せかい

a	i	u	e	o
ka	ki	ku	ke	ko
sa	**shi**	**su**	**se**	**so**
ta	chi	tsu	te	to
na	ni	nu	ne	no
ha	hi	fu	he	ho
ma	mi	mu	me	mo
ya	(i)	yu	(e)	yo
ra	ri	ru	re	ro
wa	(i)	(u)	(e)	o
n				

3. Listening Practice

3-3 ざ　じ　ず　ぜ　ぞ

4. Reading Practice

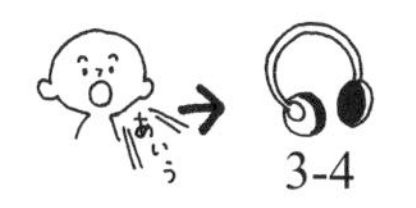
3-4

1） ざ　じ　ず　ぜ　ぞ
　　ぜ　じ　ざ　ず　ぞ

2） ごじ　かぜ　かぞく　しずか

ga	gi	gu	ge	go
za	**ji**	**zu**	**ze**	**zo**
da	ji	zu	de	do
ba	bi	bu	be	bo
pa	pi	pu	pe	po

5. Quiz

Find and circle the five hiragana letters hidden in this picture.

6. Writing Practice

								Wrong	
さ * sa	一	ャ	さ	さ					
	さ				さ				
し shi	し	し						Wrong	
	し				し				
す su	一	す	す					Wrong	
	す				す				
せ se	一	ナ	せ	せ				Wrong	
	せ				せ				
そ ** so	そ	そ						Wrong	
	そ				そ				

* さ can be also written as さ.

** そ can be also written as そ.

As shown below, *za*, *ji*, *zu*, *ze* and *zo* are written by adding two dots to さ, し, す, せ and そ.

ざ za	ざ		じ ji	じ		ず zu	ず	
ぜ ze	ぜ		ぞ zo	ぞ				

7. Let's write them once again.

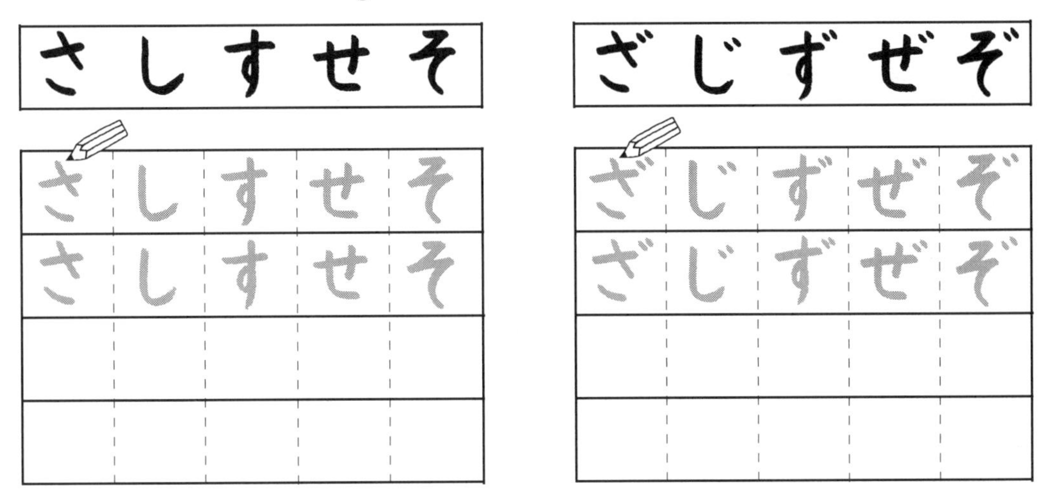

8. Let's write some words!

8. 1) kasa (umbrella) 2) shio (salt) 3) sekai (world) 4) sukoshi (a little)
5) kazoku (family)

4 たちつてと、だぢづでど

1. Listening Practice

4-1 た ち つ て と

a	i	u	e	o
ka	ki	ku	ke	ko
sa	shi	su	se	so
ta	chi	tsu	te	to
na	ni	nu	ne	no
ha	hi	fu	he	ho
ma	mi	mu	me	mo
ya	(i)	yu	(e)	yo
ra	ri	ru	re	ro
wa	(i)	(u)	(e)	o
n				

2. Reading Practice

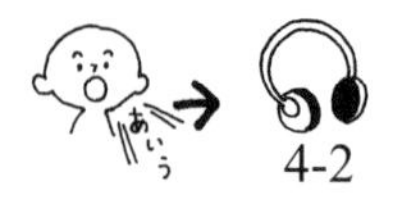

1） た　ち　つ　て　と
　　つ　ち　て　た　と

2） うた　くつ　たいせつ　ちかてつ
　　おととい

3. Listening Practice

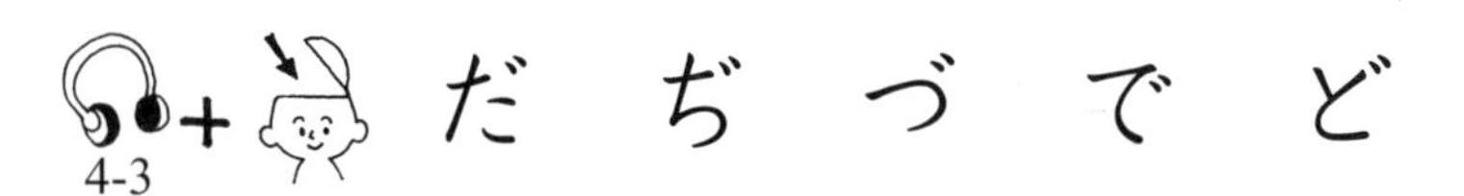

ga	gi	gu	ge	go
za	ji	zu	ze	zo
da	ji	zu	de	do
ba	bi	bu	be	bo
pa	pi	pu	pe	po

4. Reading Practice

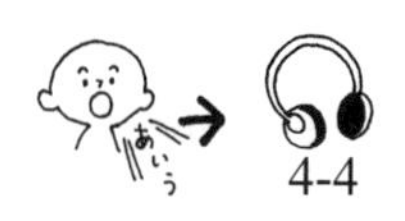

1） だ　ぢ　づ　で　ど　　ぢ　ど　で　づ　だ

2） うで　どこ　だい　かど

The pronunciation of ぢ and づ is the same as じ and ず respectively.
じ and ず are more frequently used than ぢ and づ.

5. Quiz

Connect the letters in the order of ざ, じ, ず, ぜ, ぞ and だ, ぢ, づ, で, ど.

6. Writing Practice

た ta	た				た		Wrong	
ち chi	ち				ち		Wrong	
つ tsu	つ				つ		Wrong	
て te	て				て		Wrong	
と to	と				と		Wrong	

As shown below, *da*, *ji*, *zu*, *de* and *do* are written by adding two dots to た, ち, つ, て and と.

だ da	だ		ぢ ji	ぢ			づ zu	づ		
で de	で		ど do	ど						

7. Let's write them once again.

たちつてと　だぢづでど

た	ち	つ	て	と
た	ち	つ	て	と

だ	ぢ	づ	で	ど
だ	ぢ	づ	で	ど

8. Let's write some words!

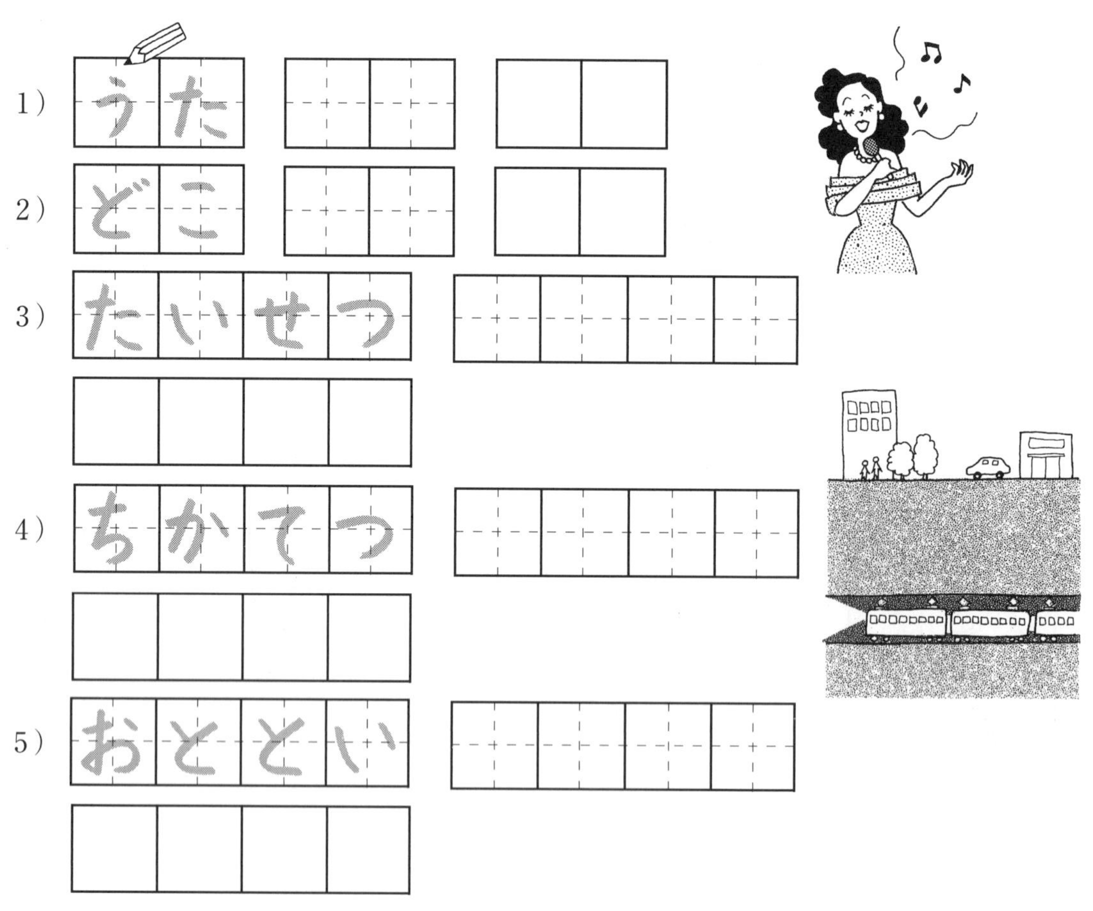

8. 1) uta (song)　2) doko (where)　3) taisetsu (important)　4) chikatetsu (subway)
5) ototoi (the day before yesterday)

Summary Practice (3 - 4)

1. Reading Practice

1) うそ　　2) うで

3) くつ　　4) じこ

5) かぜ　　6) しずか

7) ちかてつ

2. Listening and Writing Exercise

1) □□　　2) □□　　3) □□□

4) □□□　　5) □□□　　6) □□□□

7) □□□□

NOTES　Devoicing of the vowels *i* and *u*

The vowels *i* and *u* are devoiced or weakened when they occur between the voiceless consonants of *k*, *s*, *t*, *p* and *h*, or in *desu* and *masu* at the end of the sentence.

Ex.　ch/ikatetsu ちかてつ　　　k/utsu くつ

5　な　に　ぬ　ね　の

1. Listening Practice

5-1　な　に　ぬ　ね　の

a	i	u	e	o
ka	ki	ku	ke	ko
sa	shi	su	se	so
ta	chi	tsu	te	to
na	**ni**	**nu**	**ne**	**no**
ha	hi	fu	he	ho
ma	mi	mu	me	mo
ya	(i)	yu	(e)	yo
ra	ri	ru	re	ro
wa	(i)	(u)	(e)	o
n				

2. Reading Practice

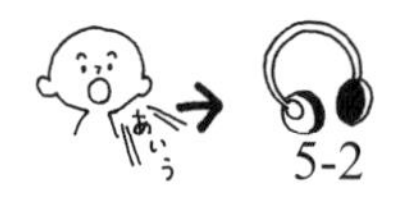

1）な　に　ぬ　ね　の
　　に　の　ぬ　ね　な

2）なつ　におい　いぬ　ねこ　のど

3. Quiz

Identify the same letter.

Ex. 1	い	(a : こ	(b): い	c : り	d : ハ)
Ex. 2	う	(a : ら	b : つ	(c): う	d : ラ)
1）	に	(a : 仁	b : しニ	c : に	d : た)
2）	の	(a : ∩	b : の	c : σ	d : 6)
3）	ね	(a : ね	b : れ	c : ぬ	d : わ)
4）	ぬ	(a : 奴	b : ぬ	c : め	d : ね)
5）	な	(a : よ	b : 奈	c : +よ	d : な)

4. Writing Practice

な na	ー	ナ	ナ゛	な	な		Wrong	
	な				な			
に ni	l	に	に	に			Wrong	
	に				に			
ぬ nu	l	ぬ	ぬ				Wrong	
	ぬ				ぬ			
ね ne	l	ね	ね				Wrong	
	ね				ね			
の no	の	の					Wrong	
	の				の			

5. Let's write them once again.

なにぬねの

な	に	ぬ	ね	の
な	に	ぬ	ね	の

6. Let's write some words!

6. 1) inu (dog) 2) neko (cat) 3) nodo (throat) 4) nani (what) 5) nioi (smell) 6) okane (money)

6　はひふへほ、ばびぶべぼ、ぱぴぷぺぽ

1. Listening Practice

6-1　は　ひ　ふ　へ　ほ

a	i	u	e	o
ka	ki	ku	ke	ko
sa	shi	su	se	so
ta	chi	tsu	te	to
na	ni	nu	ne	no
ha	**hi**	**fu**	**he**	**ho**
ma	mi	mu	me	mo
ya	(i)	yu	(e)	yo
ra	ri	ru	re	ro
wa	(i)	(u)	(e)	o
n				

2. Reading Practice

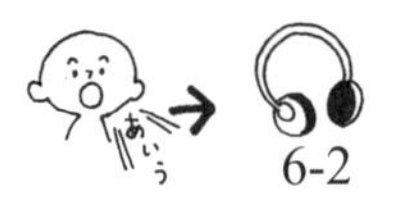

1）は　ひ　ふ　へ　ほ
　　へ　ひ　は　ふ　ほ

2）はな　ひと　ふね　ほそい　へた

3. Listening Practice

6-3　ば　び　ぶ　べ　ぼ

ga	gi	gu	ge	go
za	ji	zu	ze	zo
da	ji	zu	de	do
ba	**bi**	**bu**	**be**	**bo**
pa	pi	pu	pe	po

4. Reading Practice

1）ば　び　ぶ　べ　ぼ
　　ぶ　ぼ　べ　ば　び

2）ひび　かべ　ぼく　たばこ　かぶき

5. Listening Practice

ga	gi	gu	ge	go
za	ji	zu	ze	zo
da	ji	zu	de	do
ba	bi	bu	be	bo
pa	**pi**	**pu**	**pe**	**po**

6. Reading Practice

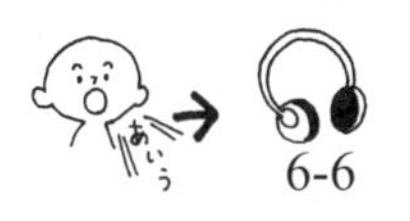

1）ぱ　ぴ　ぷ　ぺ　ぽ
　　ぴ　ぽ　ぱ　ぺ　ぷ

2）ぱちぱち　ぴかぴか　ぷかぷか　ぺたぺた　ぽきぽき

7. Quiz

6-7

Listen to the CD and circle the word you hear.

Ex. (ほかほか) ： ぽかぽか

1）	ふかふか	：	ぷかぷか	2）	ふかふか	：	ぶかぶか
3）	ひくひく	：	びくびく	4）	ぺたぺた	：	べたべた
5）	ぱたぱた	：	ばたばた	6）	ぽきぽき	：	ぼきぼき

8. Writing Practice

は ha	は	Wrong
ひ hi	ひ	Wrong
ふ fu	ふ	Wrong
へ he	へ	Wrong
ほ ho	ほ	Wrong

As shown below, *ba*, *bi*, *bu*, *be* and *bo* are written by adding two dots to は, ひ, ふ, へ and ほ.

ば ba	ば	び bi	び	ぶ bu	ぶ
べ be	べ	ぼ bo	ぼ		

As shown below, *pa*, *pi*, *pu*, *pe* and *po* are written by adding a small circle to the top right-hand side of は, ひ, ふ, へ and ほ.

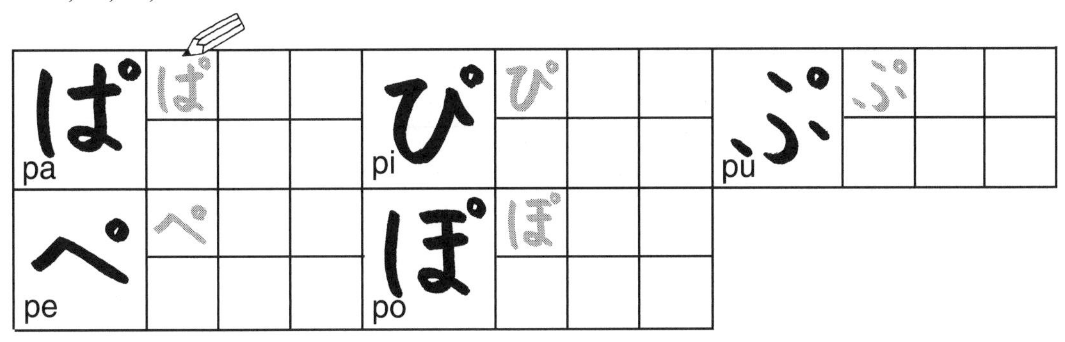

9. Let's write them once again.

は	ひ	ふ	へ	ほ
は	ひ	ふ	へ	ほ
は	ひ	ふ	へ	ほ

ば	び	ぶ	べ	ぼ
ば	び	ぶ	べ	ぼ

ぱ	ぴ	ぷ	ぺ	ぽ
ぱ	ぴ	ぷ	ぺ	ぽ

10. Let's write some words!

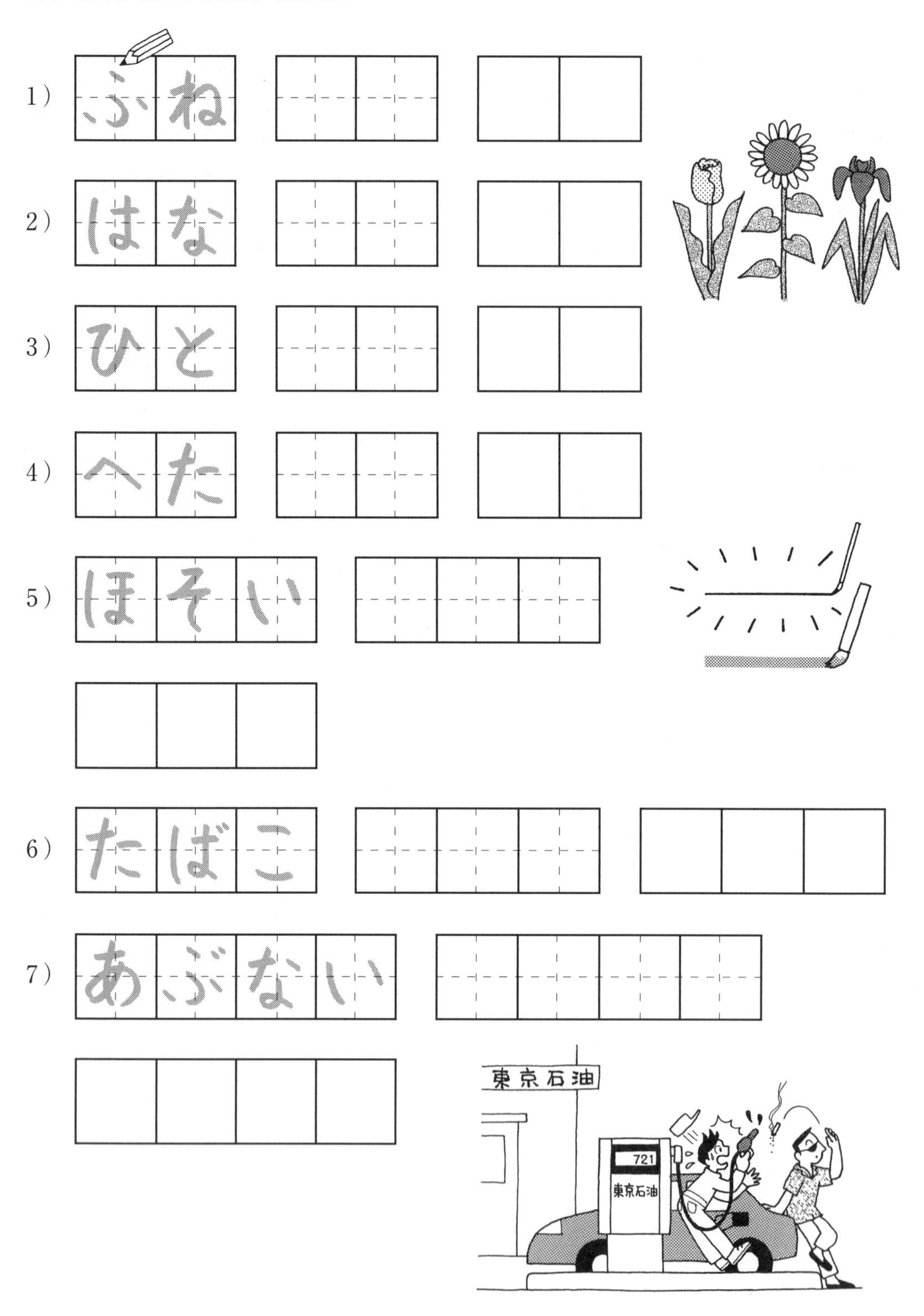

10. 1) fune (ship) 2) hana (flower) 3) hito (person) 4) heta (be poor at)
5) hosoi (thin) 6) tabako (tobacco) 7) abunai (dangerous)

Summary Practice (5 - 6)

1. Reading Practice

1) はな　2) いぬ　3) ふね

4) なに　5) ぼく*　6) のど

7) たばこ　8) こいびと

9) かぶき　10) ぽかぽか

* ぼく may be also pronounced as ぼく .

2. Listening and Writing Exercise

1) □□　2) □□　3) □□

4) □□　5) □□□　6) □□□

7) □□□□

7 まみむめも、やゆよ

1. Listening Practice

7-1 まみむめも

a	i	u	e	o
ka	ki	ku	ke	ko
sa	shi	su	se	so
ta	chi	tsu	te	to
na	ni	nu	ne	no
ha	hi	fu	he	ho
ma	mi	mu	me	mo
ya	(i)	yu	(e)	yo
ra	ri	ru	re	ro
wa	(i)	(u)	(e)	o
n				

2. Reading Practice

1） ま　み　む　め　も
　　む　め　も　ま　み

2） みず　あめ　なまえ　むすこ
　　のみもの

3. Listening Practice

7-3 やゆよ

a	i	u	e	o
ka	ki	ku	ke	ko
sa	shi	su	se	so
ta	chi	tsu	te	to
na	ni	nu	ne	no
ha	hi	fu	he	ho
ma	mi	mu	me	mo
ya	(i)	yu	(e)	yo
ra	ri	ru	re	ro
wa	(i)	(u)	(e)	o
n				

4. Reading Practice

1） や　ゆ　よ　よ　ゆ　や

2） やま　ゆき　よみかた　ふゆ

5. Quiz

Find and circle the following hiragana words in the box.

Ex.	いま	ima
1）	やま	yama
2）	ゆき	yuki
3）	あめ	ame
4）	およぐ	oyogu
5）	さむい	samui
6）	ともだち	tomodachi

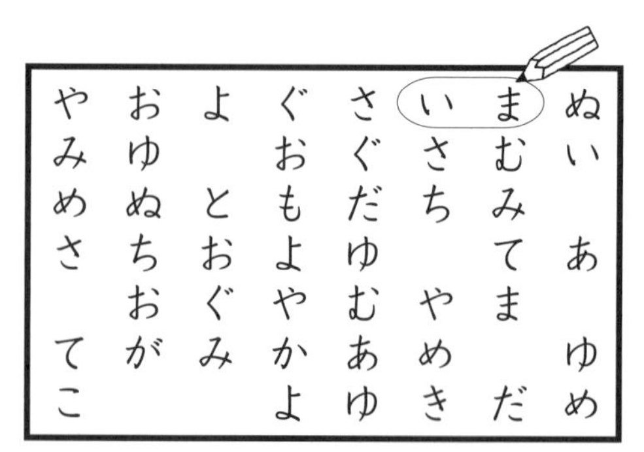

や	お	よ	ぐ	さ	い	ま	ぬ
み	ゆ		お	ぐ	さ	む	い
め	ぬ	と	も	だ	ち	み	
さ	ち	お	よ	ゆ		て	あ
	お	ぐ	や	む	や	ま	
て	が	み	か	あ	め		ゆ
こ			よ	ゆ	き	だ	め

---

5. Ex. now　1) mountain　2) snow　3) rain　4) swim　5) cold, chilly　6) friend

6. Writing Practice

								Wrong	
ま ma	ま	ま	ま	ま					
	ま				ま				
み mi	み	み	み					Wrong	
	み				み				
む mu	む	む	む	む				Wrong	
	む				む				
め me	め	め	め					Wrong	
	め				め				
も mo	も	も	も	も				Wrong	
	も				も				

								Wrong	
や ya	や	や	や	や					
	や				や				
ゆ yu	ゆ	ゆ	ゆ					Wrong	
	ゆ				ゆ				
よ yo	よ	よ	よ					Wrong	
	よ				よ				

7. Let's write them once again.

8. Let's write some words!

8. 1) yama (mountain) 2) ame (rain) 3) yuki (snow) 4) mizu (water)
5) musume (daughter) 6) nomimono (drink) 7) yomi-kata (how to read)

8 ら り る れ ろ、わ、を、ん

1. Listening Practice

8-1 ら り る れ ろ

a	i	u	e	o
ka	ki	ku	ke	ko
sa	shi	su	se	so
ta	chi	tsu	te	to
na	ni	nu	ne	no
ha	hi	fu	he	ho
ma	mi	mu	me	mo
ya	(i)	yu	(e)	yo
ra	**ri**	**ru**	**re**	**ro**
wa	(i)	(u)	(e)	o*
n				

2. Reading Practice

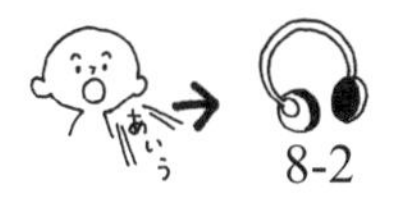

1） ら り る れ ろ
　　れ り ら る ろ

2） ひる どれ いくら ひだり
　　しろい

3. Listening Practice

8-3 わ を ん

a	i	u	e	o
ka	ki	ku	ke	ko
sa	shi	su	se	so
ta	chi	tsu	te	to
na	ni	nu	ne	no
ha	hi	fu	he	ho
ma	mi	mu	me	mo
ya	(i)	yu	(e)	yo
ra	ri	ru	re	ro
wa	**(i)**	**(u)**	**(e)**	**o***
n				

4. Reading Practice

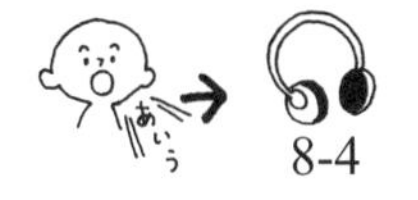

1） わ を ん を ん わ

2） わたしも りんごを* たべます

*Though を has the same pronunciation as お, the way it is used is different. を is a particle and always used together with a noun. (See page 50 for more examples.)

5. Quiz

Find and circle the following hiragana words in the box.

Ex.	なまえ	namae
1）	どれ	dore
2）	よる	yoru
3）	いくら	ikura
4）	ひだり	hidari
5）	わたし	watashi

み	ろ	ひ	だ	り	わ	た	と
ち	よ	る	つ	ひ	ど	れ	ね
よ	ろ	め		ど	わ	た	し
わ	な	ま	え	ぬ	ど	わ	よ
り	と	れ	い	く	ら	の	れ

5. Ex. name　1) which one　2) night　3) how much　4) left (side)　5) I

6. Writing Practice

								Wrong
ら ra	ら	ら	ら					
	ら				ら			
り ri	り	り	り					Wrong
	り				り			
る ru	る	る						Wrong
	る				る			
れ re	れ	れ	れ					Wrong
	れ				れ			
ろ ro	ろ	ろ						Wrong
	ろ				ろ			

								Wrong
わ wa	わ	わ	わ					
	わ				わ			
を o	を	を	を	を				Wrong
	を				を			
ん n	ん	ん						Wrong
	ん				ん			

7. Let's write them once again.

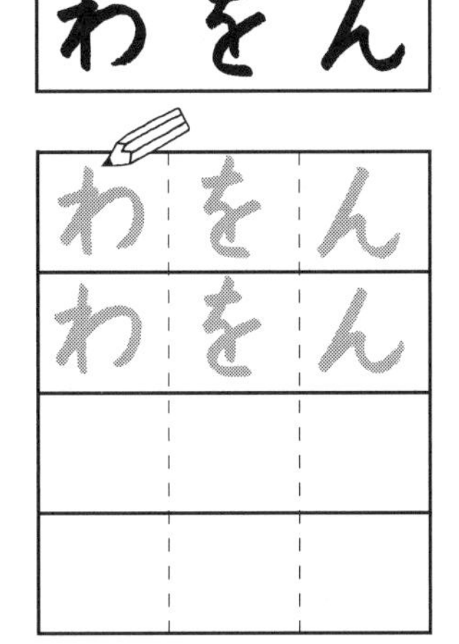

らりるれろ　　わをん

8. Let's write some words!

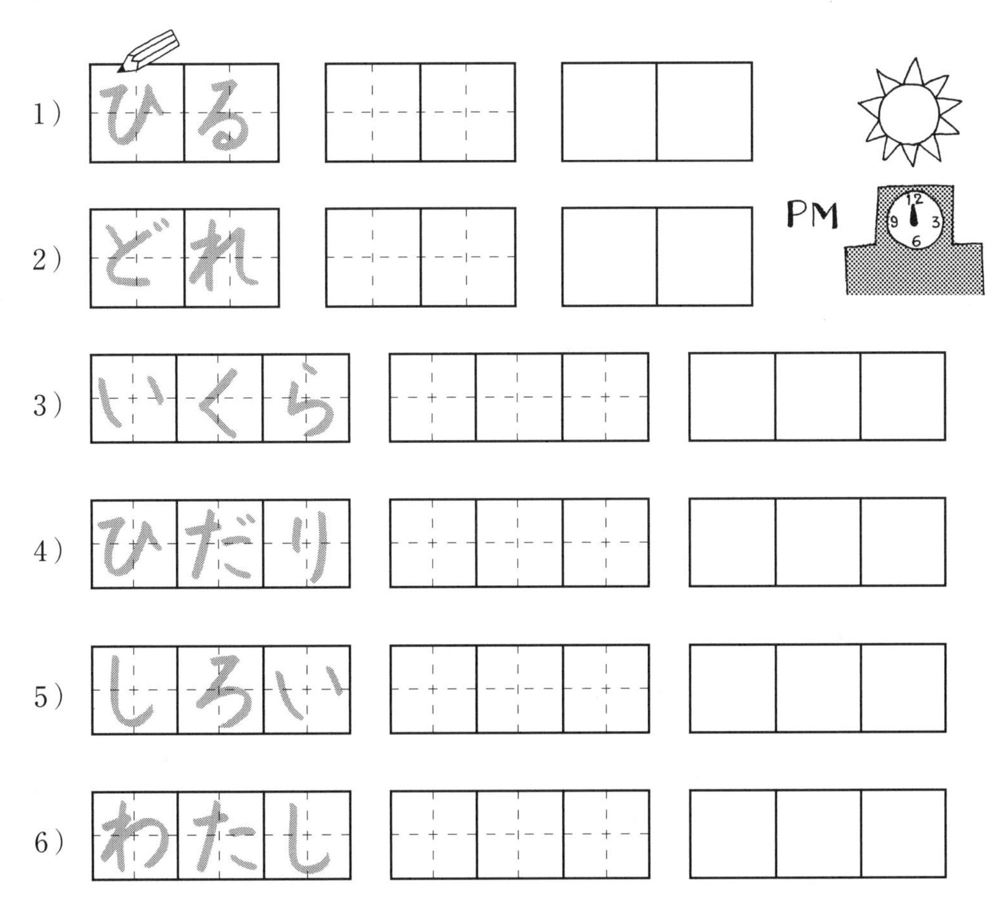

8. 1) hiru (day time, noon) 2) dore (which one) 3) ikura (how much)
4) hidari (left [side]) 5) shiroi (white) 6) watashi (I)

Summary Practice (7 - 8)

1. Reading Practice

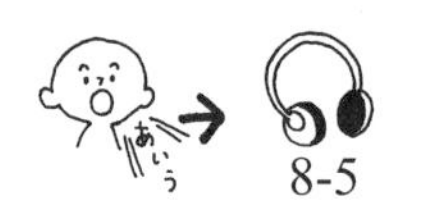

1) やま　2) よる　3) どれ

4) あめ　5) ゆき　6) むすこ

7) いくら　8) わたし

9) みかん　10) ともだち

2. Listening and Writing Exercise

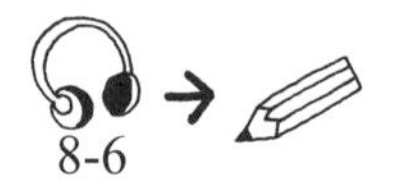

1) □□　2) □□　3) □□

4) □□□　5) □□□　6) □□□

7) □□□　8) □□□　9) □□□□

10) □□□□

Let's Check!

The empty boxes below represent hiragana letters which are often confused by students. Write down the correct hiragana letters in these boxes.

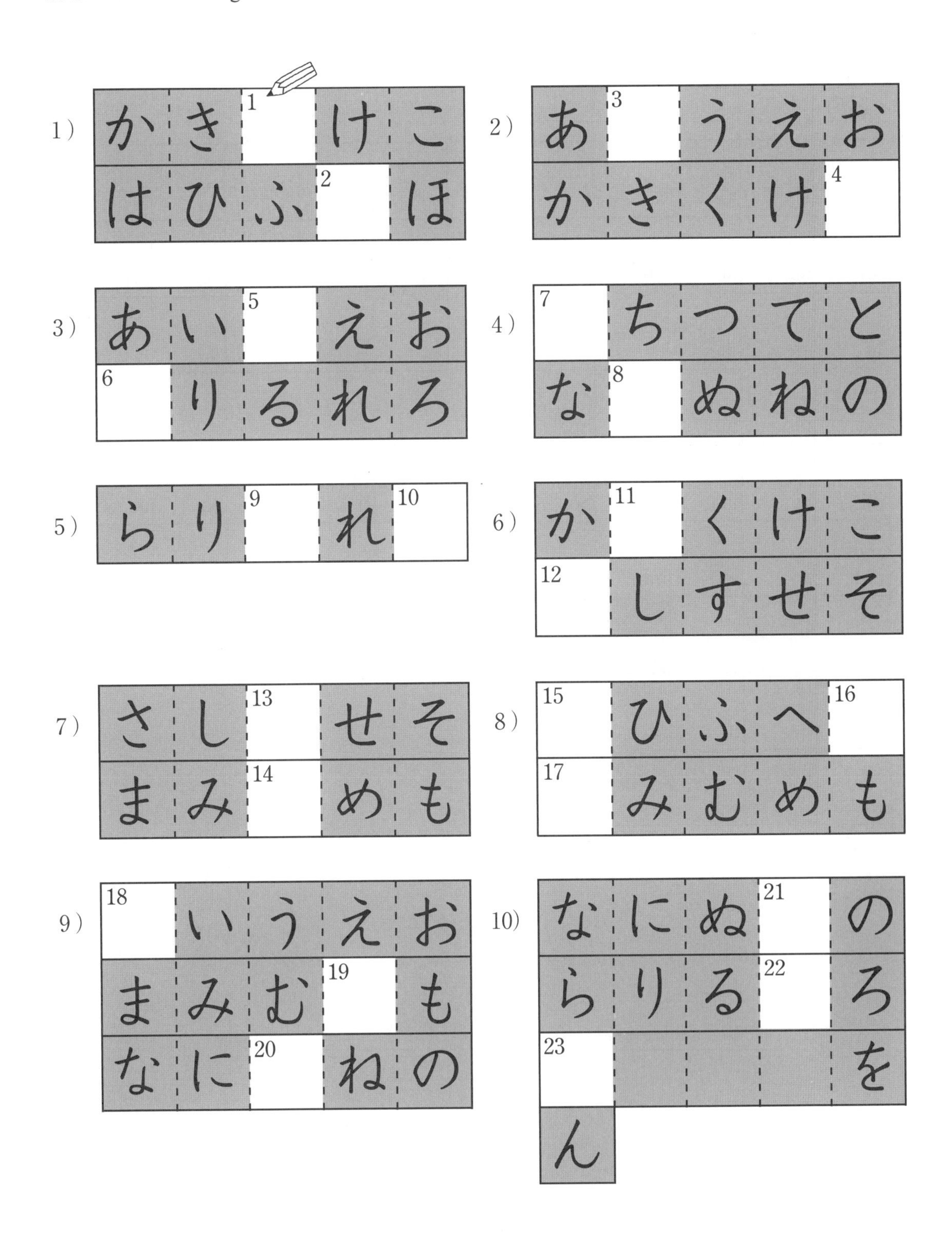

Test 1

Complete the hiragana list.

a あ	i	u	e	o
ka	ki	ku	ke	ko
sa	shi	su	se	so
ta	chi	tsu	te	to
na	ni	nu	ne	no
ha	hi	fu	he	ho
ma	mi	mu	me	mo
ya		yu		yo
ra	ri	ru	re	ro
wa				o
n ん				

ga	gi	gu	ge	go
za	ji	zu	ze	zo
da	ji	zu	de	do

ba	bi	bu	be	bo
pa	pi	pu	pe	po

Test 2

tesuto 2
(Test 2)

Listen to the CD and write down the words in hiragana in the boxes.

1） 2） 3） 4）

5） 6） 7） 8）

9） 10） 11） 12）

13） 14） 15） 16）

17） 18） 19） 20）

Column 3 Japanese Types of Print

Japanese letters sometimes look different depending on the typefaces used to print them. Some letters printed in certain typefaces look like other letters because of the difference in the thickness of the line and / or the design of the strokes at the beginning or at the end. Also, there are letters whose shapes have changed because some of their strokes are connected.

A myriad number of typefaces have come to be used in the last 10 to 20 years. Many unique and eye-catching print styles often appear in magazines, advertisements, street billboards, etc. You may have a chance to see them.

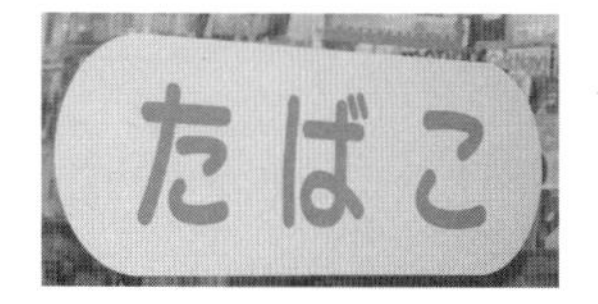

Below are some different typefaces. Study them carefully and see what makes them look different.

かきくけこ　さしすせそ　はひふへほ

かきくけこ　さしすせそ　はひふへほ

かきくけこ　さしすせそ　はひふへほ

かきくけこ　さしすせそ　はひふへほ

かきくけこ　さしすせそ　はひふへほ

9 Long Vowels

1. Listening Practice

9-1

	short vowel			long vowel
obasan (aunt)	おばさん	:	obāsan (grandmother)	おばあさん
ojisan (uncle)	おじさん	:	ojiisan (grandfather)	おじいさん
yuki (snow)	ゆき	:	yūki (courage)	ゆうき
e (picture)	え	:	ē (yes)	ええ
heya (room)	へや	:	heiya (plain)	へいや
koko (here)	ここ	:	kōkō (high school)	こうこう
toru (take)	とる	:	tōru (pass along)	とおる

In the first example, "*ba*" (ば) in *obasan* has a short sound, while "*bā*" (ばあ) in *obāsan* has a long sound. When the length of the sound is different, the meaning of the word is also different. The following table shows how to write letters with long vowel sounds in hiragana.

short sound		hiragana that is added		long sound examples
あ か が さ ざ た だ な は ば ぱ ま や ら わ	+	あ	→	かあ、さあ
い き ぎ し じ ち ぢ に ひ び ぴ み り	+	い	→	きい、しい
う く ぐ す ず つ づ ぬ ふ ぶ ぷ む ゆ る	+	う	→	くう、すう
え け げ せ ぜ て で ね へ べ ぺ め れ	+	い／え*	→	けい、せい、ねえ
お こ ご そ ぞ と ど の ほ ぼ ぽ も よ ろ	+	う／お*	→	こう、そう、とお

* In the case of long voweled え or お, it is rather unusual to use え or お in writing. い instead of え and う instead of お are usually used.

2. Quiz

9-2 Listen to the CD and circle the word you think you hear.

Ex. ここ：(こうこう)

1）ま：まあ　2）い：いい　3）ふ：ふう　4）ね：ねえ

5）と：とお　6）も：もう　7）ほし：ほしい　8）くろ：くろう

9）ゆめ：ゆうめい　10）こてい：こうてい

3. Let's write some words!

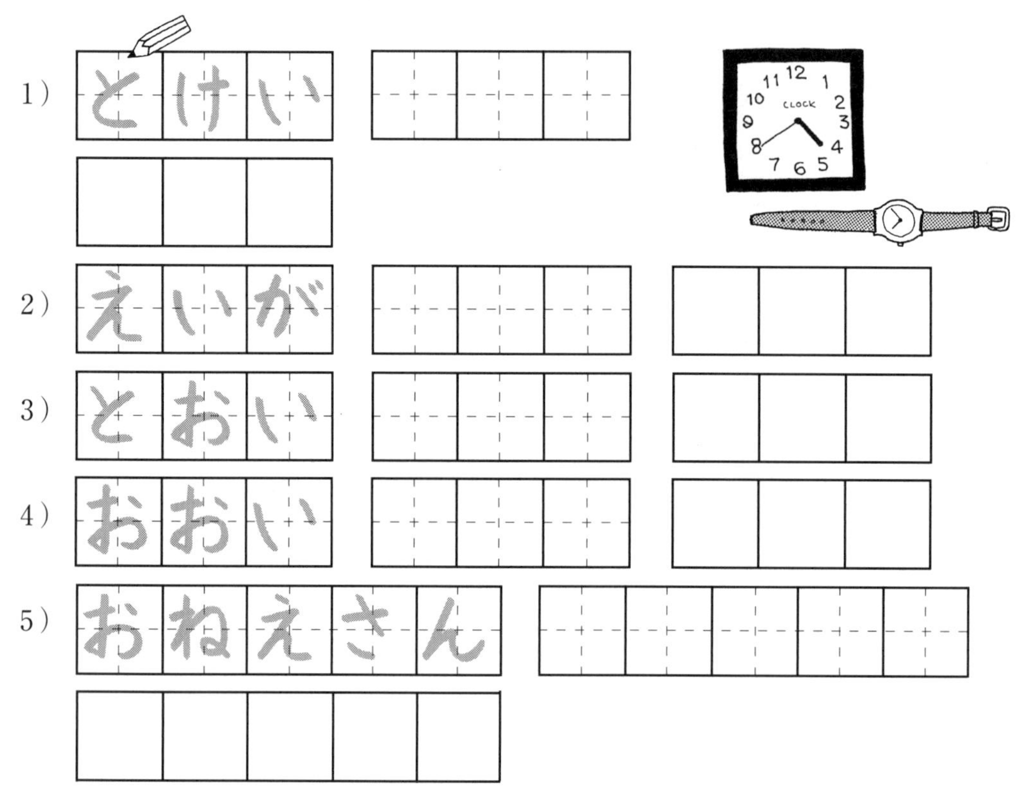

3. 1) tokei (watch, clock)　2) eiga (movie)　3) tōi (far)　4) ōi (many)
5) onēsan (elder sister)

4. Listening and Writing Exercise

9-3

Listen to the CD and write the correct letters in the boxes.
Either え or お should be put in the box with ＊.

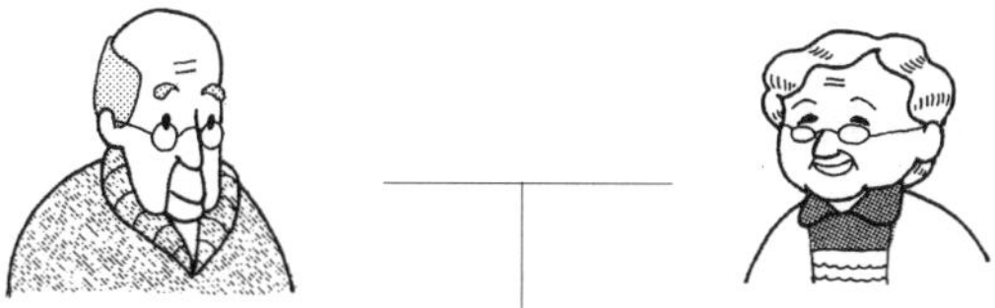

1. 1）お□□さん　2）お□□さん

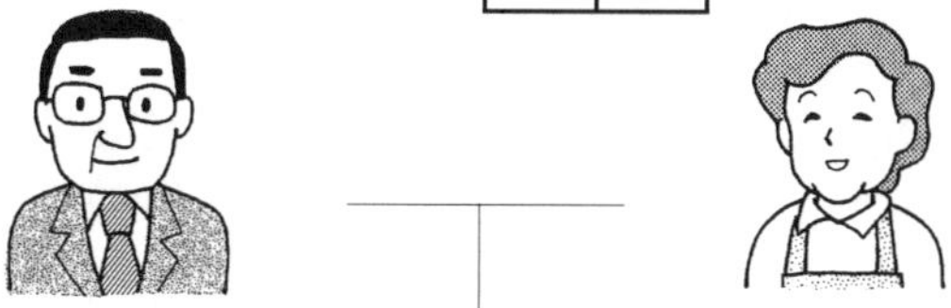

3）お□□さん　4）お□□さん

5）お□□さん　6）お□□＊さん　わたし　7）い□□と　8）お□□と

9-4

2. 1）□□□□　2）□□□□　3）□□□

4）□□＊□　5）□□□　6）□□□□

10 Small Size っ

1. Listening Practice

Listen to the CD carefully to check the difference between the sounds of the words on the left and the words on the right.

kako (past)	かこ	:	kakko (parenthesis)	かっこ
isai (details)	いさい	:	issai (one year old)	いっさい
oto (sound)	おと	:	otto (husband)	おっと
ichi (one)	いち	:	itchi (agreement)	いっち

Have you been able to distinguish the difference?
Compare the words written in hiragana. The words on the right have a small っ in them. This is not pronounced at all; it merely denotes a breathless pause made for the length of the pronunciation of one letter.

This small っ should be used to transcribe the first consonant of *kk*, *ss*, *tt* and *tch*, as is shown in the example of the romanized words above, as well as some other letters such as *pp* (ex. *kippu* きっぷ ticket). However, this small っ should not be used for the transcription of *nn* (ex. *donna* どんな what kind of).

2. Reading Practice

Read the following words carefully, paying attention to っ.
Then listen to the CD to check the pronunciation.

1）きて、きって	2）いて、いって	3）もと、もっと
4）かき、かっき	5）ぴたり、ぴったり	6）きっぷ
7）みっつ	8）どっち	9）あさって
10）ゆっくり		

3. Let's write some words!

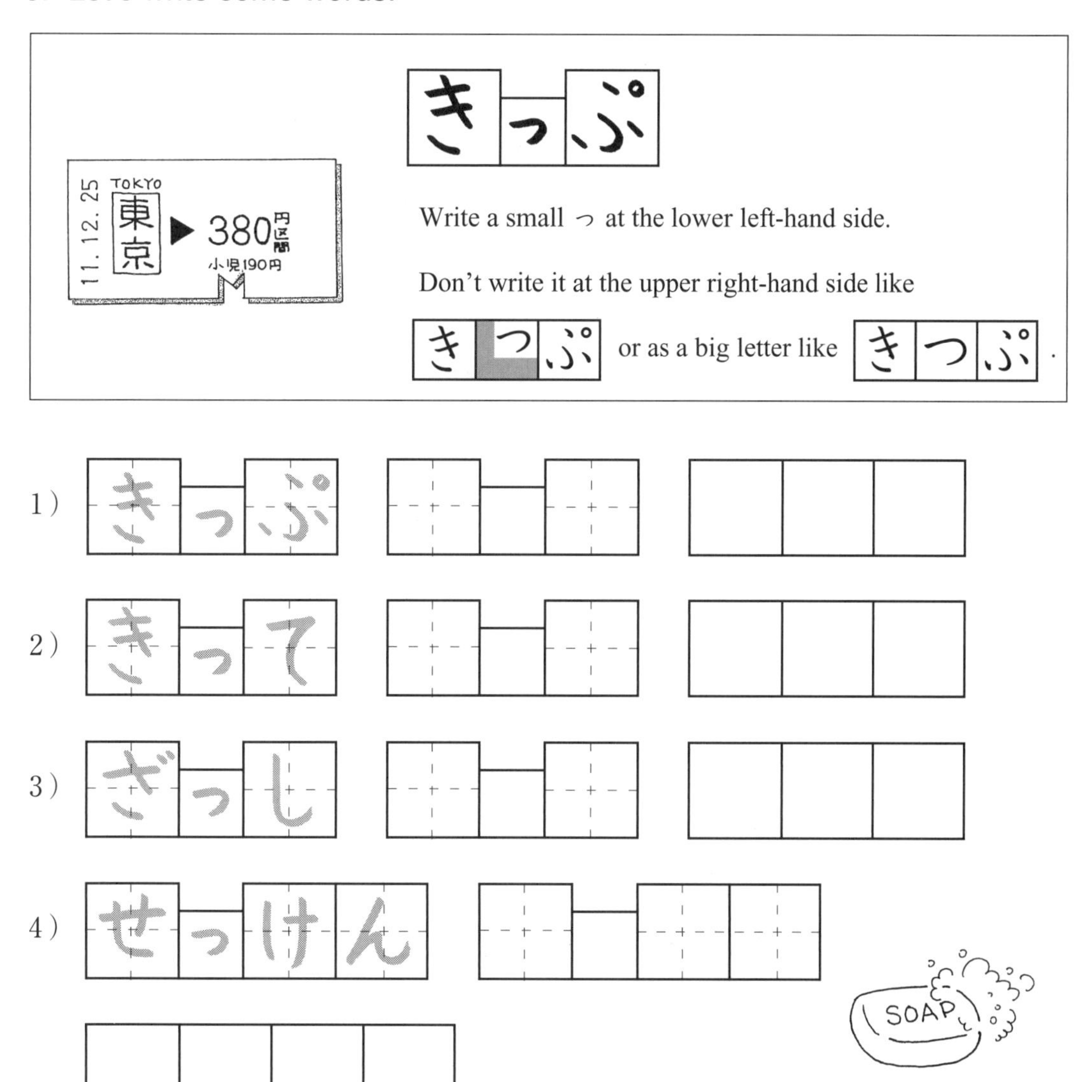

4. Listening and Writing Exercise

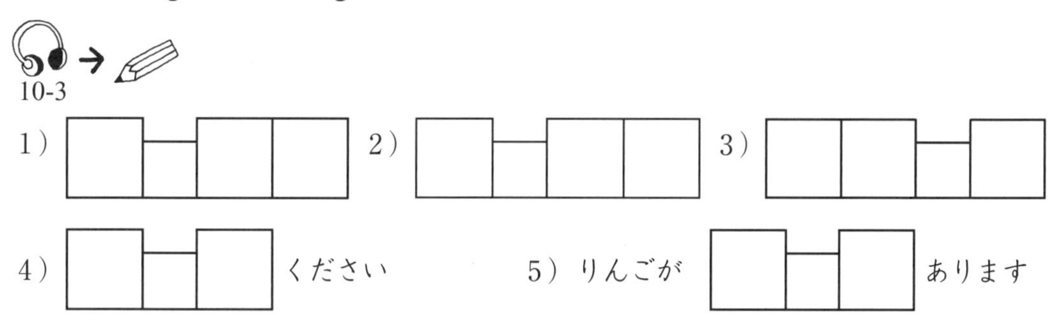

3. 1) kippu (ticket) 2) kitte (stamp) 3) zasshi (magazine) 4) sekken (soap)

11 きゃ、きゅ、きょ

1. Listening Practice

11-1

Listen to the CD carefully to check the difference between the sounds of the words on the left and the words on the right.

hiyaku (leap, jump)	ひやく	:	hyaku (one hundred)	ひゃく
kashiya (house for rent)	かしや	:	kasha (freight train)	かしゃ

Each hiragana letter in the words on the left side is pronounced individually, as in ひ や く, while in the case of the words on the right, ひゃ should be pronounced as one sound, like ひゃ く. These sounds are denoted by a smaller than normal size ゃ, ゅ and ょ.

2. Reading Practice

Listen to the pronunciation while looking at the following letters. Then pronounce them by yourself.

①

きゃ	きゅ	きょ
kya	kyu	kyo
しゃ	しゅ	しょ
sha	shu	sho
ちゃ	ちゅ	ちょ
cha	chu	cho
にゃ	にゅ	にょ
nya	nyu	nyo
ひゃ	ひゅ	ひょ
hya	hyu	hyo

②

みゃ	みゅ	みょ
mya	myu	myo
りゃ	りゅ	りょ
rya	ryu	ryo

③

ぎゃ	ぎゅ	ぎょ
gya	gyu	gyo
じゃ	じゅ	じょ
ja	ju	jo

④

びゃ	びゅ	びょ
bya	byu	byo
ぴゃ	ぴゅ	ぴょ
pya	pyu	pyo

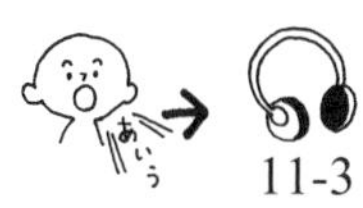

Read the following words carefully, paying attention to ○ゃ, ○ゅ and ○ょ.

1）じしょ　　2）おちゃ　　3）ひゃく

4）かいしゃ　　5）しゅくだい

3. Writing Practice

As with a small っ, when ○ゃ, ○ゅ or ○ょ is written, it should be written at the lower left-hand side at half the normal size.

①

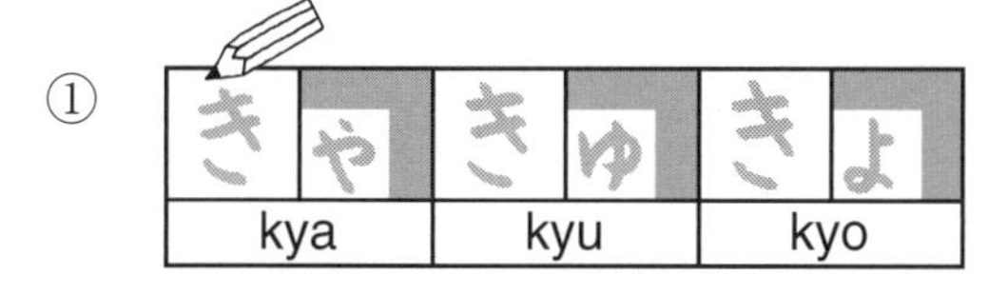

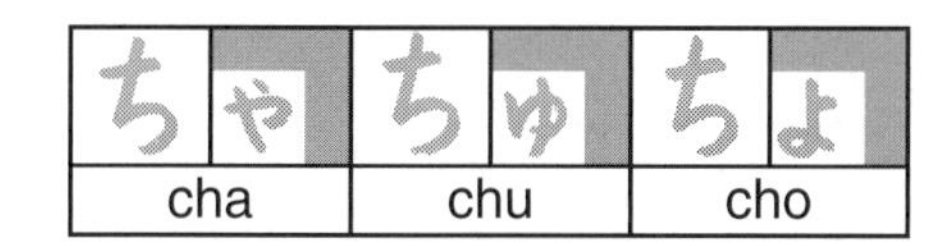

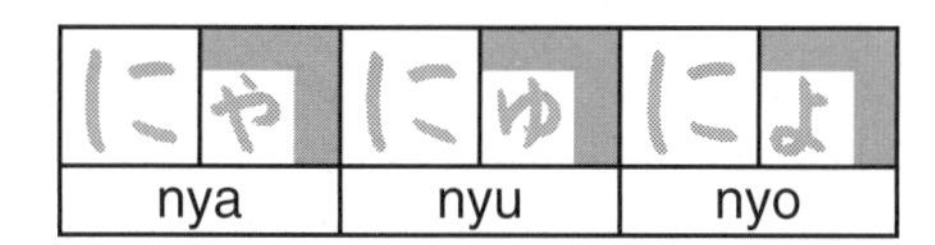

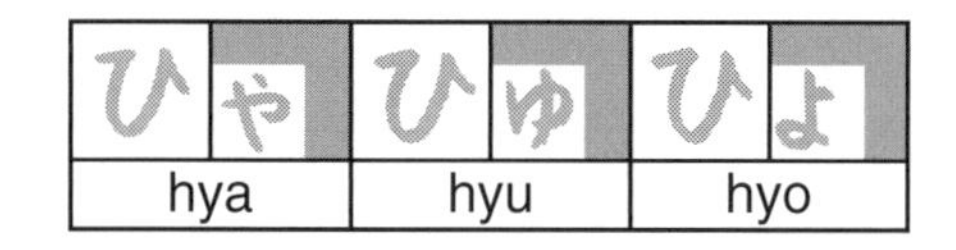

②

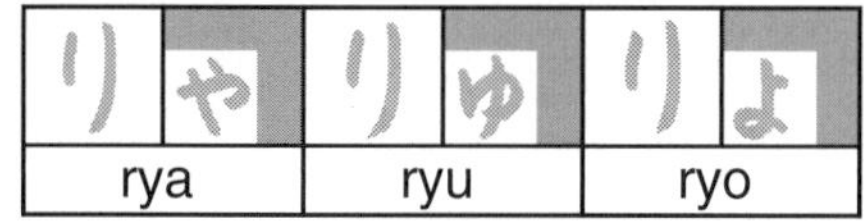

③

ぎゃ	ぎゅ	ぎょ
gya	gyu	gyo

じゃ	じゅ	じょ
ja	ju	jo

④

びゃ	びゅ	びょ
bya	byu	byo

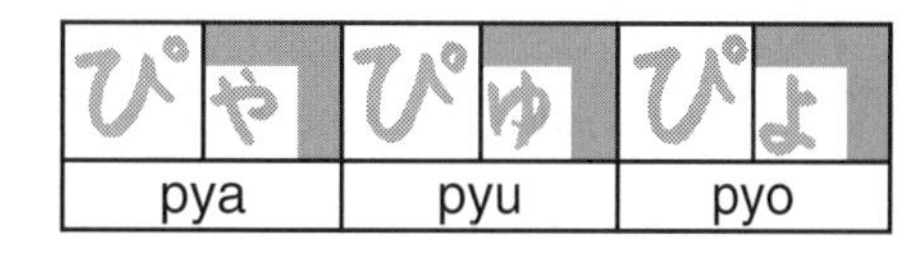

4. Let's write some words!

4. 1) jisho (dictionary) 2) ocha (tea) 3) hyaku (one hundred) 4) kyonen (last year)
5) shukudai (homework)

きゃあ、きゅう、きょう

The long vowel forms of ○ゃ, ○ゅ and ○ょ are written ○ゃあ, ○ゅう and ○ょう (お is not used).

1. Reading Practice

11-4

①

きゃあ	きゅう	きょう
kyā	kyū	kyō
しゃあ	しゅう	しょう
shā	shū	shō
ちゃあ	ちゅう	ちょう
chā	chū	chō
にゃあ	にゅう	にょう
nyā	nyū	nyō
ひゃあ	ひゅう	ひょう
hyā	hyū	hyō

②

みゃあ	みゅう	みょう
myā	myū	myō
りゃあ	りゅう	りょう
ryā	ryū	ryō

③

ぎゃあ	ぎゅう	ぎょう
gyā	gyū	gyō
じゃあ	じゅう	じょう
jā	jū	jō

④

びゃあ	びゅう	びょう
byā	byū	byō
ぴゃあ	ぴゅう	ぴょう
pyā	pyū	pyō

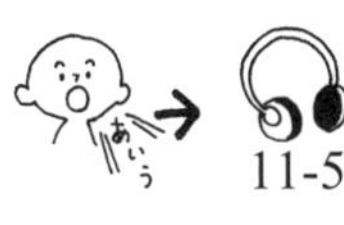
11-5

Read the following words carefully, paying attention to ○ゅう and ○ょう.

1）きよう、きょう　　2）びよういん、びょういん

3）べんきょう　　4）ちゅうごく　　5）ぎゅうにゅう

2. Writing Practice

As with a small っ, when ○ゃ, ○ゅ or ○ょ is written, it should be written at the lower left-hand side at half the normal size.

3. Let's write some words!

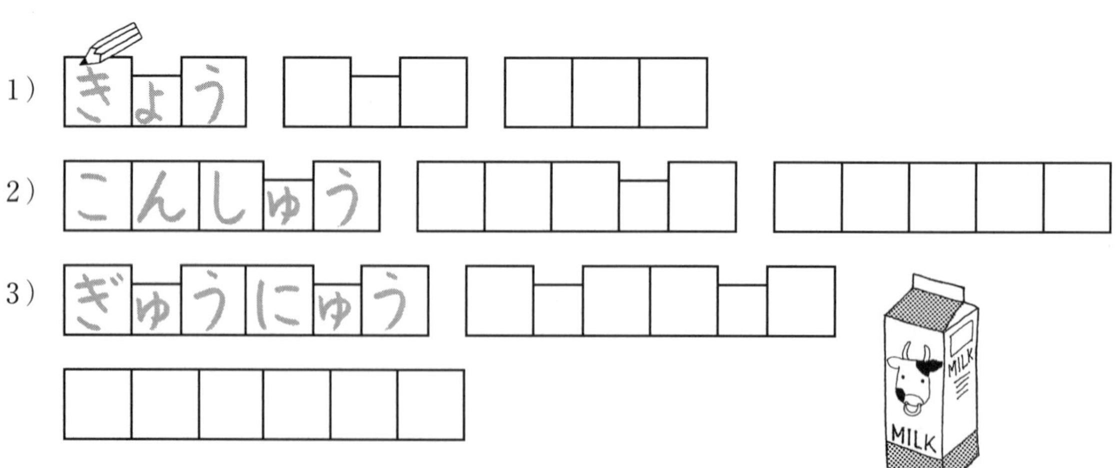

3. 1) kyō (today) 2) konshū (this week) 3) gyūnyū (milk)

きゃっ、きゅっ、きょっ

There are some cases in which a small っ comes after ○ゃ, ○ゅ or ○ょ.

1. Listening Practice

chotto (a little)	ちょっと	juppun (ten minutes)	じゅっぷん
shutchō (business trip)	しゅっちょう		

2. Let's write some words!

1）
2）
3）

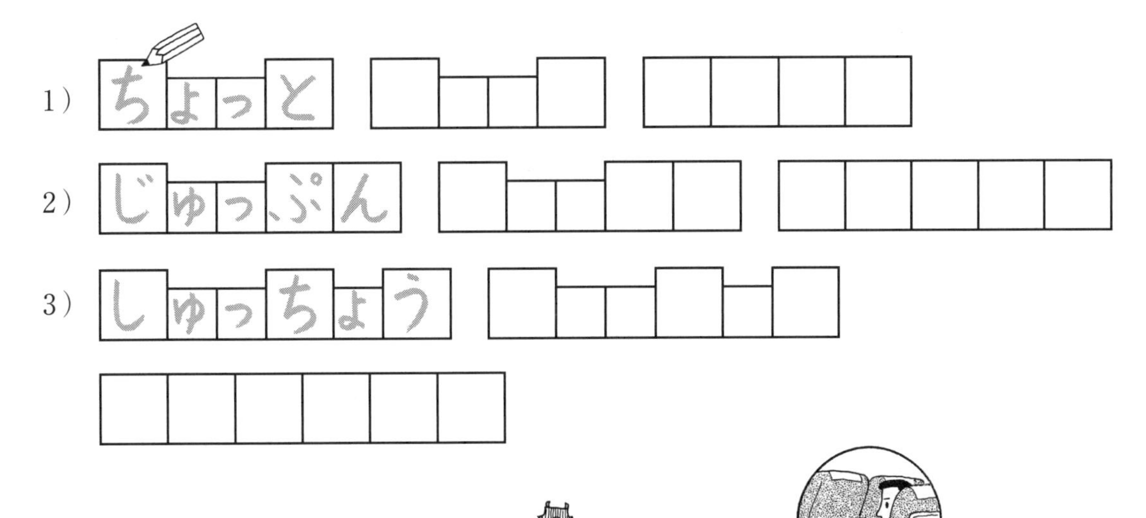

Summary Practice (9 - 11)

1. Reading Practice

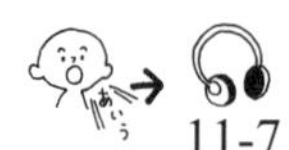

1） とけい

2） おはよう

3） ざっし

4） あさって

5） おちゃ

6） きょう

7） かいしゃ

8） ぎゅうにゅう

2. Listening and Writing Exercise

1）

2）

3）

4）

5）

6）

7）

8）

9）

10）

12 Usage of は, へ and を in Sentences

は [wa]・へ [e]・を [o]

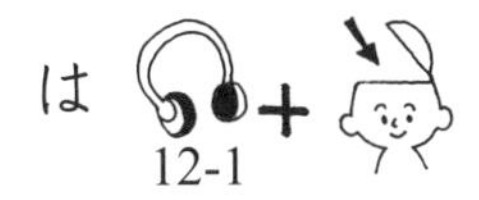

Examples

1）わたしは　けんしゅうせいです。　I'm a trainee.

Watashi wa kenshūsei desu.

2）わたしは　にほんじんでは　ありません。　I'm not Japanese.

Watashi wa Nihon-jin dewa arimasen.

3）こんにちは。　Good afternoon.

Konnichiwa.

Ex. 1)
は is usually pronounced [ha]. But when it is used as a particle, it is pronounced [wa].

Ex. 2) & Ex. 3)
When は in では　ありません and は in こんにちは are written, は is commonly used instead of わ.

Examples

1）きのう　にほんへ　きました。　(I) came to Japan yesterday.

Kinō Nihon e kimashita.

2）らいねん　くにへ　かえります。(I) go back to (my) country next year.

Rainen kuni e kaerimasu.

3）ぎんこうへ　いきます。　(I) go to the bank.

Ginkō e ikimasu.

へ is usually pronounced [he]. But when it is used as a particle, it is pronounced [e].

NOTES

A particle functions as a link between words to make a sentence.

Example ①　かいしゃ (company)　いきます (go)

Example ②　かいしゃへ (to the company)　いきます。(go)　((I) go to the company.)

In example ①, two words are merely put side by side. But in example ②, when the particle へ is added to the word meaning "company", the relationship between the two words becomes clear.

を 

Examples

1）ほんを　よみます。　　(I) read a book.

Hon o yomimasu.

2）にほんごを　べんきょうします。　　(I) study Japanese.

Nihon-go o benkyō-shimasu.

Both お and を are pronounced [o]. But を is used only as a particle, while お is never used in that way.

Sentences Written in Hiragana

Examples

1）わたしは　けんしゅうせいです。　　I am a trainee.

Watashi wa kenshūsei desu.

2）わかりませんから、ゆっくり　はなして　ください。　　As I can't understand, please speak slowly.

Wakarimasen kara, yukkuri hanashite kudasai.

3）かのじょは「あなたが　すき」といった。　　She said, "I love you."

Kanojo wa anata ga suki to itta.

At the end of a sentence, the mark "。" is used as a period. As can be seen in example 2), "、" is used like a comma to punctuate in the middle of a sentence. As for the positions of "。" and "、", they are written at the bottom when written horizontally. "「 」" are used as quotation marks, as can be seen in example 3).

1. Reading Practice

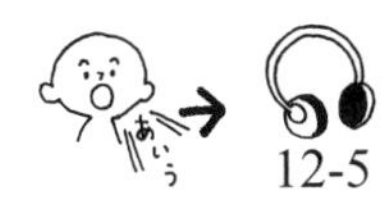

1）わたしは　すずきです。

2）せんせいでは　ありません。

3）ざっしを　よみます。

4）かいしゃへ　いきます。

5）こんばんは。

2. Listening and Writing Exercise

Example: わたしは　たなか　です。

1）＿＿＿＿＿＿　がくせい　＿＿＿＿＿＿＿＿＿＿＿＿

2）＿＿＿＿＿＿＿＿＿＿＿＿＿＿＿＿＿＿　いきます。

3）＿＿＿＿＿＿＿＿＿＿＿＿＿＿＿＿＿＿　ください。

4）＿＿＿＿＿＿＿＿＿＿＿＿＿＿＿＿＿＿＿＿＿＿＿

5）＿＿＿＿＿＿＿＿＿＿＿＿＿＿＿＿＿＿＿＿＿＿＿

6）＿＿＿＿＿＿＿＿＿＿＿＿＿＿＿＿＿＿＿＿＿＿＿

---

1. 1) Watashi wa Suzuki desu.	I'm Suzuki.
2) Sensei dewa arimasen.	(I) am not a teacher.
3) Zasshi o yomimasu.	(I) read a magazine.
4) Kaisha e ikimasu.	(I) go to the company.
5) Konbanwa.	Good evening.

Vertical Writing

So far, you have studied how to write horizontally. Japanese, however, can be also written vertically. Most newspapers and novels are written in this way. Vertically written sentences start at the top of the right-hand side.

Ex. horizontal writing vertical writing

①しんぶん

②きっぷ

③しゃちょう

How to write vertically

A small っ, like in example ② きっぷ, and small ゃ and ょ, like in example ③ しゃちょう, should be written at the upper right-hand side when written vertically.

As for the positions of "。" and "、", they are written at the upper right-hand side as well, when written vertically. "「 」" are used as quotation marks as in example C.

Vertical Writing Example

A わたしは けんしゅうせいです。

B わかりませんから、ゆっくり はなして ください。

C かのじょは「あなたが すき」といった。

3. Writing Practice

Ex. きっぷ

1）せっけん

2）かいしゃ

3）ぎゅうにゅう

4）おげんきですか。

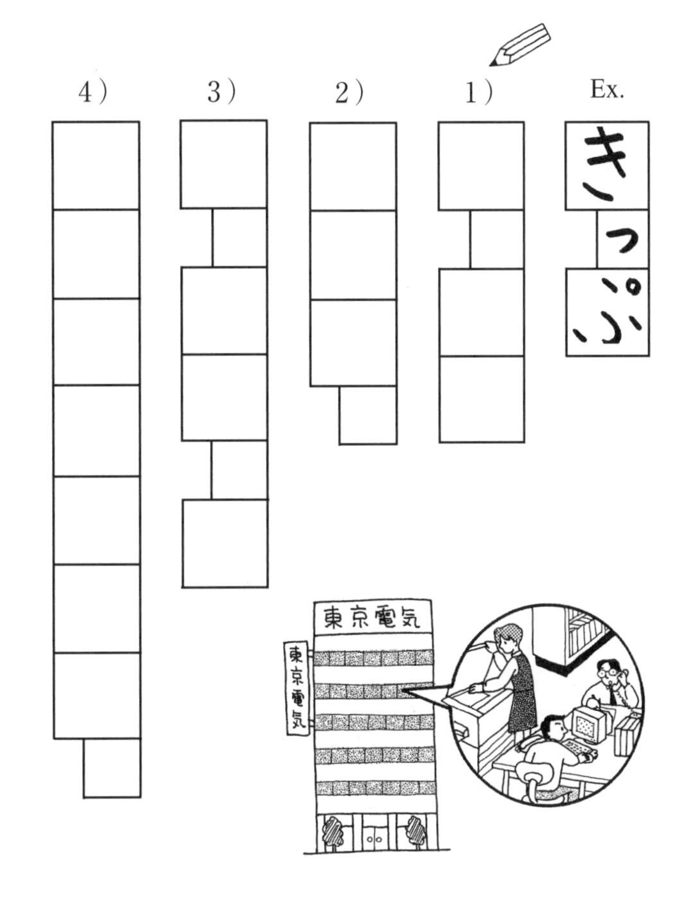

---

3. Ex. kippu (ticket) 1) sekken (soap) 2) kaisha (company) 3) gyūnyū (milk)
4) O-genki desu ka. (How are you?)

Crossword Puzzles

Do the following crossword puzzles, using the words you have learned so far. If you have not yet remembered all the words, listen to the CD and fill in the boxes.

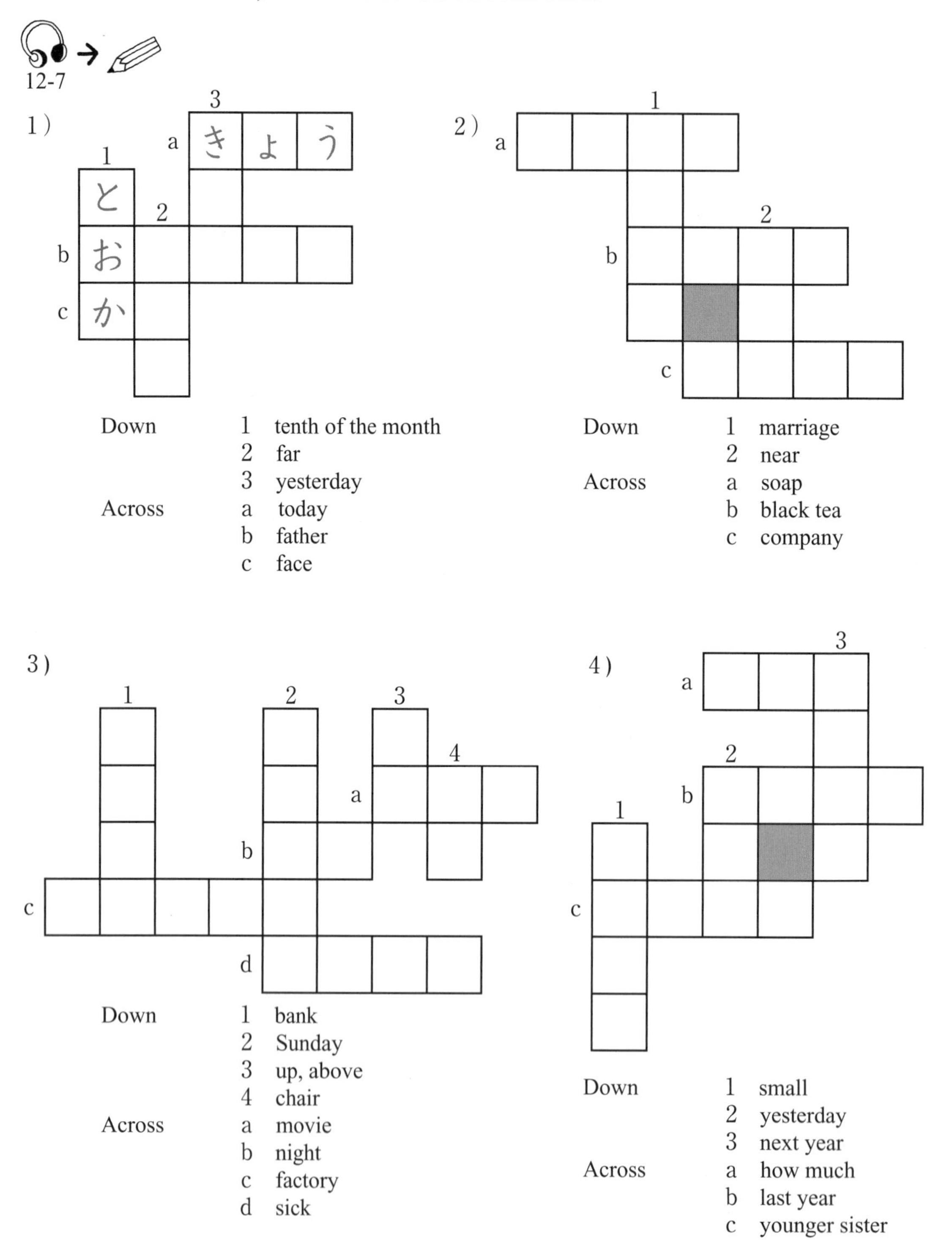

1)

Down
1 tenth of the month
2 far
3 yesterday

Across
a today
b father
c face

2)

Down
1 marriage
2 near

Across
a soap
b black tea
c company

3)

Down
1 bank
2 Sunday
3 up, above
4 chair

Across
a movie
b night
c factory
d sick

4)

Down
1 small
2 yesterday
3 next year

Across
a how much
b last year
c younger sister

Test 3

1．Listen to the CD and write down the words or sentences.

1）

2）

3）

4）

5）

6）

7）

8）

9）

10） くださいｏ

2．This is a letter to Mr. Tanaka from Mr. Narong. Listen to the CD and write down what is said.

5がつ23にち

1）

2）

3）

4）

5）

Narong

Column 4 Origin of Kana

In ancient times, when no writing system had yet been developed in Japan, Japanese people tried to use kanji from China, which was a nation of advanced culture and learning, to write the Japanese language. Since Chinese and Japanese are totally different in pronunciation, however, it was difficult to adopt the kanji as they were to express the sounds used in Japanese.

Hiragana letters were thus developed to record the sounds used in Japanese in written form, by modifying and simplifying kanji to make them easy for everyone to write. They have a round shape. Katakana letters, on the other hand, were derived from a part of kanji, and they are comprised of straight lines and angles. Both writing systems were created some 1,000 years ago.

Example of the development of hiragana:

安 → 安 → 安 → あ

Example of the development of katakana:

阿 → 阝 → ア → ア

Origin of hiragana

あ安	い以	う宇	え衣	お於
か加	き幾	く久	け計	こ己
さ左	し之	す寸	せ世	そ曽
た太	ち知	つ川	て天	と止
な奈	に仁	ぬ奴	ね祢	の乃
は波	ひ比	ふ不	へ部	ほ保
ま末	み美	む武	め女	も毛
や也		ゆ由		よ与
ら良	り利	る留	れ礼	ろ呂
わ和				を遠
ん无				

Origin of katakana

ア阿	イ伊	ウ宇	エ江	オ於
カ加	キ幾	ク久	ケ介	コ己
サ散	シ之	ス須	セ世	ソ曽
タ多	チ千	ツ川	テ天	ト止
ナ奈	ニ仁	ヌ奴	ネ祢	ノ乃
ハ八	ヒ比	フ不	ヘ部	ホ保
マ末	ミ三	ム牟	メ女	モ毛
ヤ也		ユ由		ヨ与
ラ良	リ利	ル流	レ礼	ロ呂
ワ和				ヲ乎
ンレ				

引用　日本語教育学会編，日本語教育事典，大修館書店

PART II

KATAKANA

か　　　　た　　　　か　　　　な

Katakana words in the pictures

テレビ　terebi (television)

ビデオ　bideo (video)

パソコン　pasokon (personal computer)

コインロッカー　koin-rokkā (coin-operated locker)

カレーライス　karē raisu (curry and rice)

ラーメン　rāmen (Chinese noodles in soup)

ホームページ　アドレス　hōmupēji-adoresu (homepage address)

13 ア　イ　ウ　エ　オ、ン

Words Written in Katakana

1) Words of foreign origin, and names of foreign places, people and things:
   Ex. カメラ (camera), インド (India), ラオさん (Mr. Rao)
2) Words that express sounds (onomatopoeic words), and words that express states and conditions (mimetic words):
   Ex. トントン (knock knock), ガタガタ (rattle)
3) Words that a writer wants to emphasize:
   Ex. ビックリ！ (surprise)

Names of animals and plants are also frequently written in katakana.

Features of Katakana Letters

Hiragana is mainly made of curved lines, while katakana consists of straight lines and angles.

Although katakana ン (n) is the very last kana in the kana table, it appears in the first section, because it is very frequently used in words written in katakana.

To assist your studies, the order of katakana practices is somewhat different from the hiragana practices in this workbook.

Now, let's begin.

1. Listening Practice

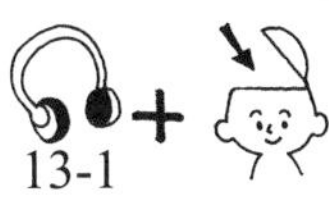

Try to remember the shapes of the following letters while listening to their pronunciation.

ア	イ	ウ	エ	オ	ン
あ	い	う	え	お	ん

2. Reading Practice

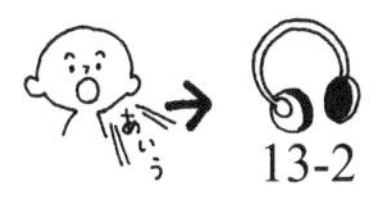

Read aloud the following letters. Then listen to the CD.

イ　オ　エ　ン　ア　ウ

3. Writing Practice

ア あ	ア	ア	ア				Wrong
	ア			ア			
イ い	イ	イ	イ				Wrong
	イ			イ			
ウ う	ウ	ウ	ウ	ウ			Wrong
	ウ			ウ			
エ え	エ	エ	エ	エ			Wrong
	エ			エ			
オ お	オ	オ	オ	オ			Wrong
	オ			オ			
ン ん	ン	ン	ン				Wrong
	ン			ン			

4. Let's write them once again.

First, trace the lightly written letters. Then write them by yourself.

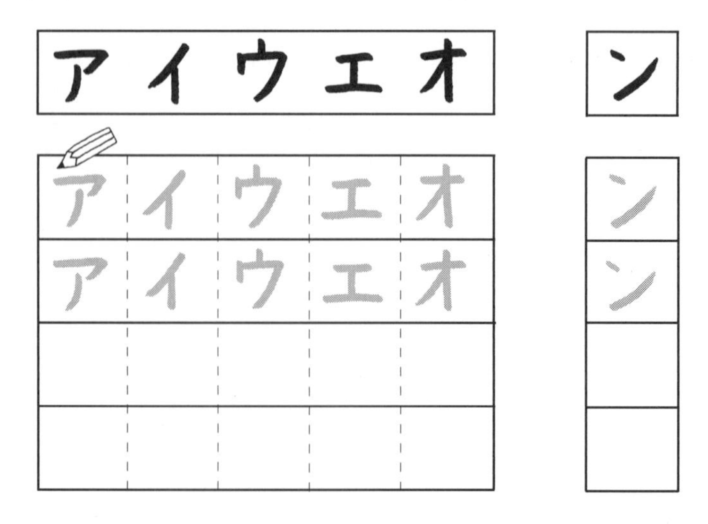

5. Write the katakana letters that correspond to the hiragana letters.

え	お	ん	あ	う	い	え
エ						

6. Let's write some words!

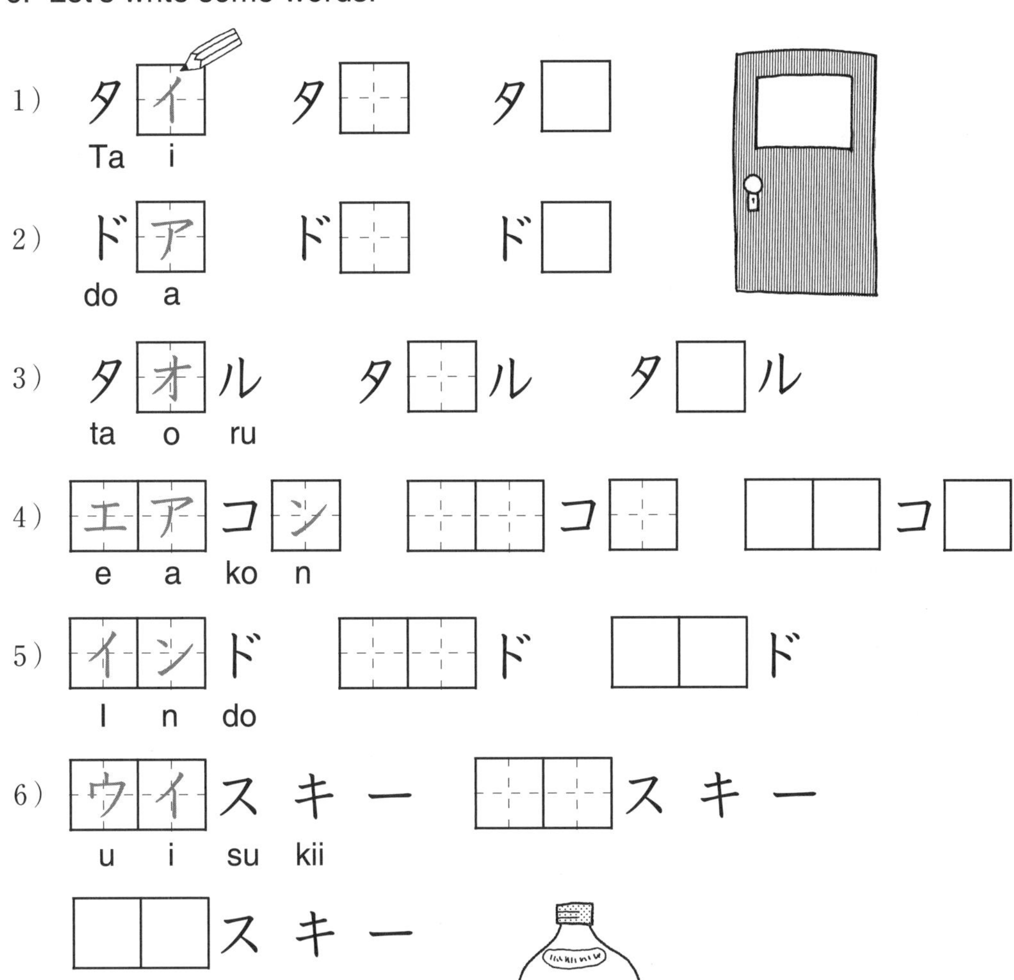

---

6. 1) Tai (Thailand) 2) doa (door) 3) taoru (towel) 4) eakon (air-conditioner)
5) Indo (India) 6) uisukii (whiskey)

14 カ キ ク ケ コ、ガ ギ グ ゲ ゴ

1. Listening Practice

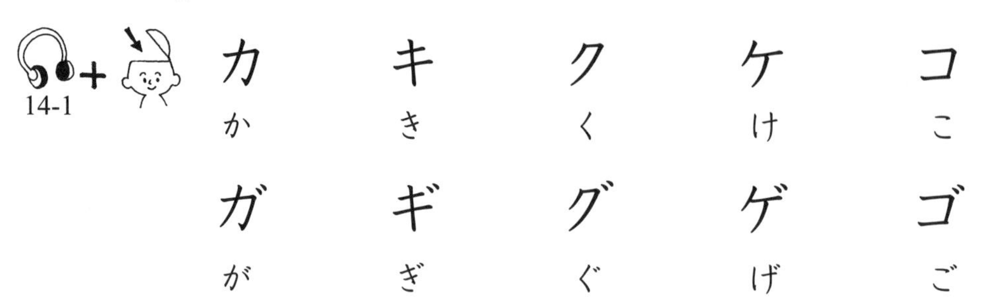

カ	キ	ク	ケ	コ
か	き	く	け	こ
ガ	ギ	グ	ゲ	ゴ
が	ぎ	ぐ	げ	ご

2. Reading Practice

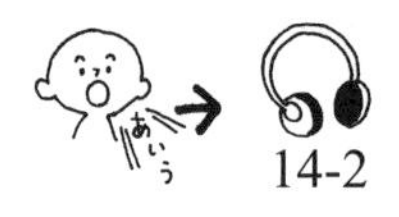

1） ク　コ　キ　カ　ケ　　ギ　グ　ゲ　ゴ　ガ

2） エアコン

3. Writing Practice

カ か	フ	カ	カ				Wrong
	カ			カ			か
キ き	ー	ニ	キ	キ			Wrong
	キ			キ			き
ク く	ク	ク	ク				Wrong
	ク			ク			ワ

ケ
け

コ
こ

Wrong

Wrong

As shown below, *ga*, *gi*, *gu*, *ge* and *go* are written by adding two dots to カ, キ, ク, ケ and コ.

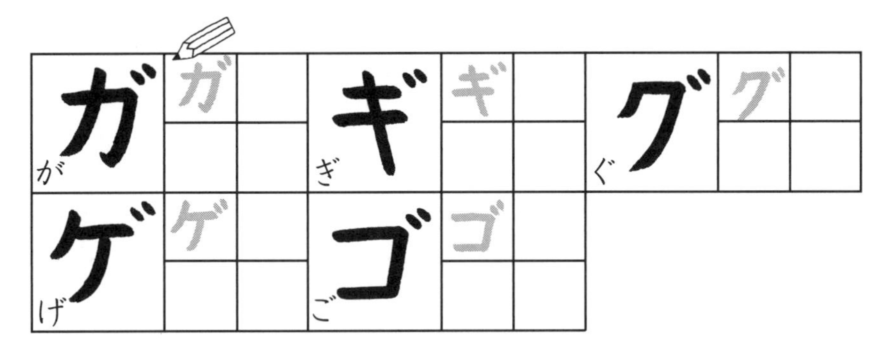

4. Let's write them once again.

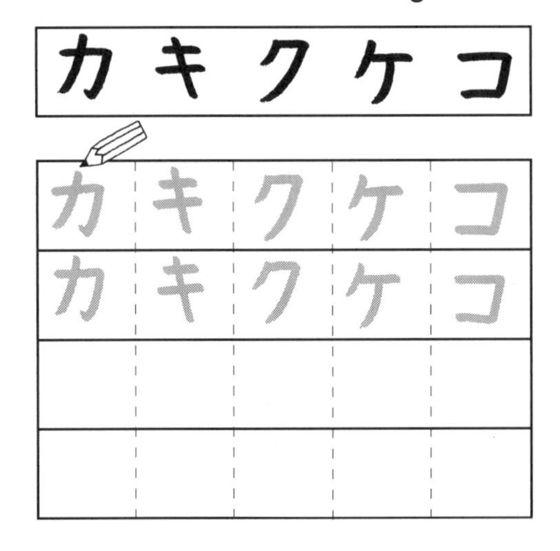

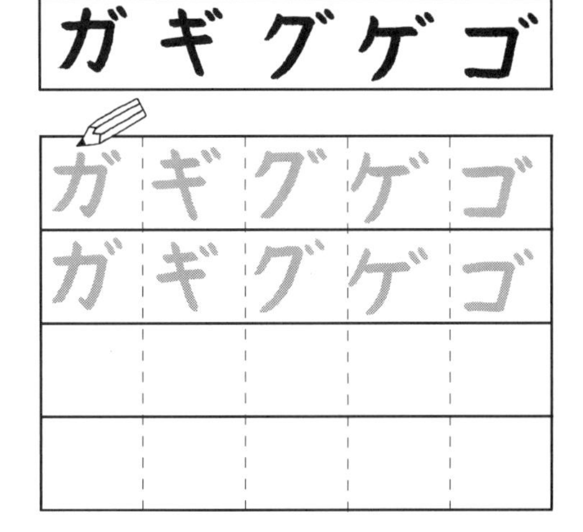

5. Write the katakana letters that correspond to the hiragana letters.

ぐ	こ	き	が	げ	ご	く	か	ぎ	け	ぐ
グ										

6. Let's write some words!

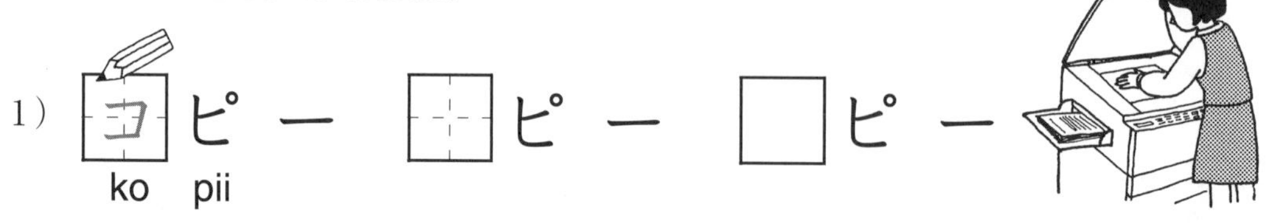

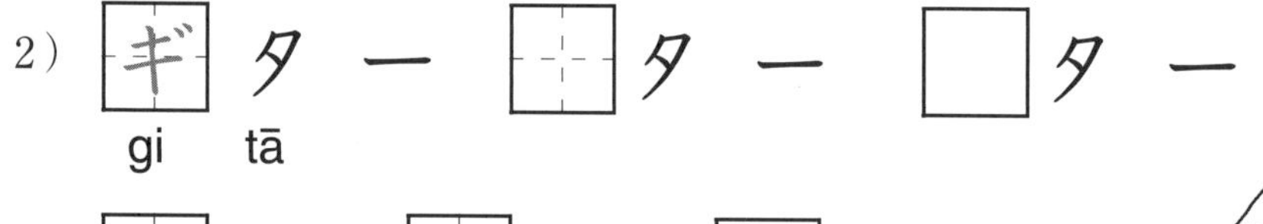

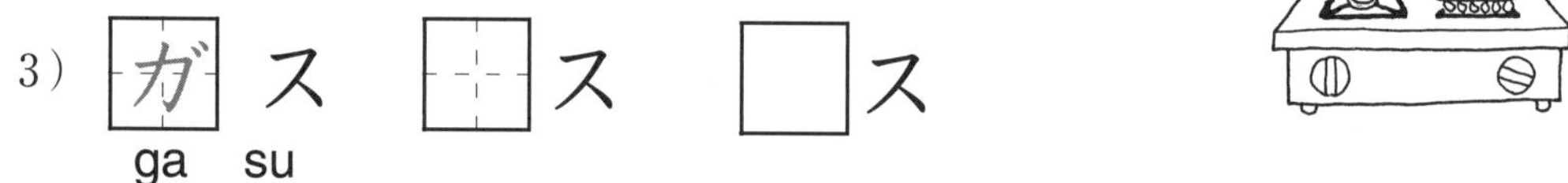

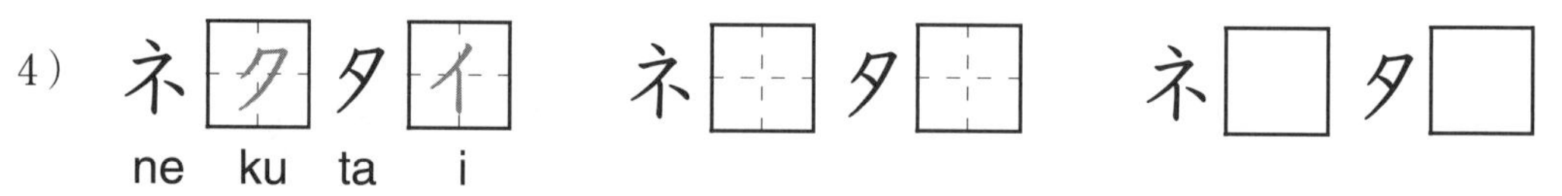

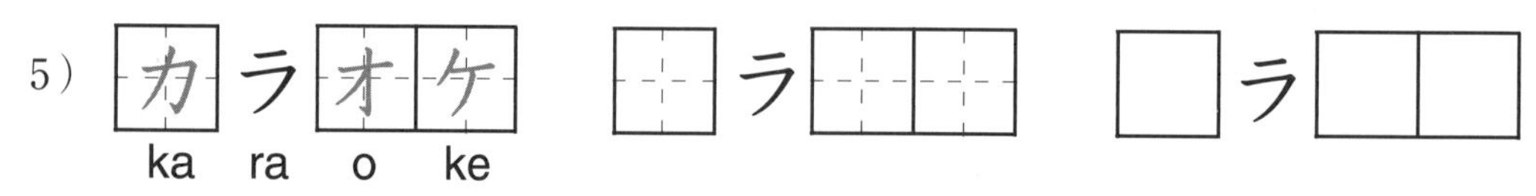

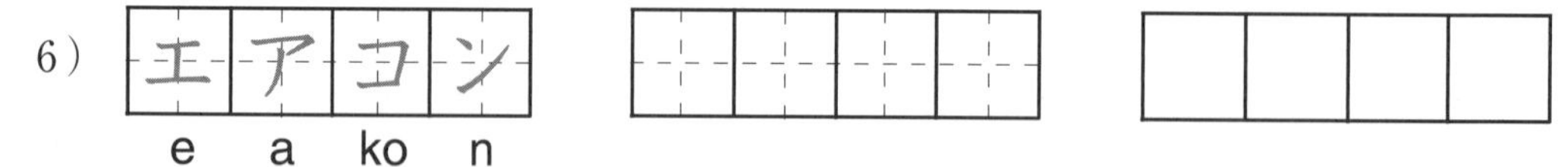

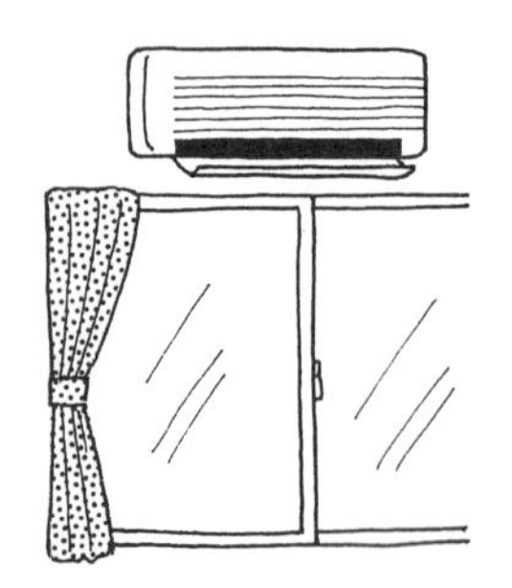

6. 1) kopii (copy) 2) gitā (guitar) 3) gasu (gas) 4) nekutai (necktie)
5) karaoke (a sing-along machine) 6) eakon (air-conditioner)

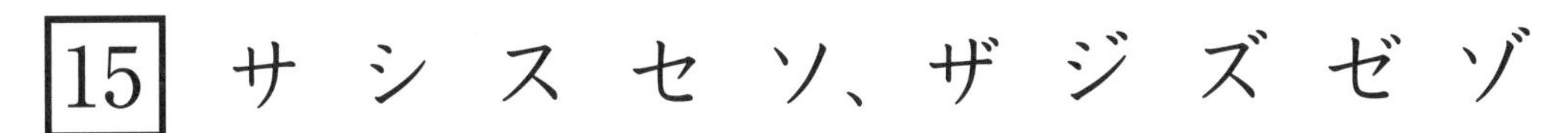

15 サ シ ス セ ソ、ザ ジ ズ ゼ ゾ

1. Listening Practice

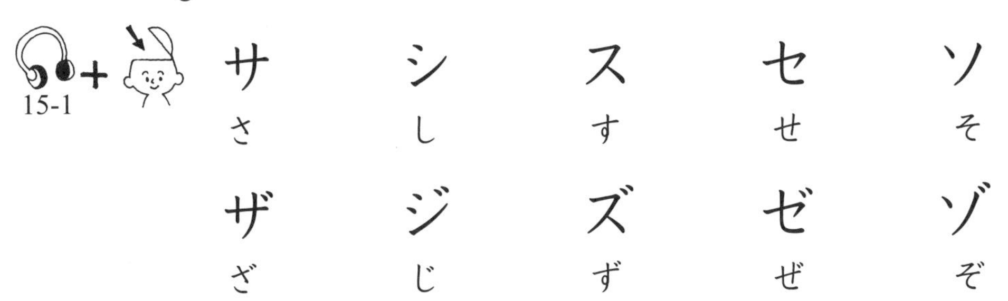

2. Reading Practice

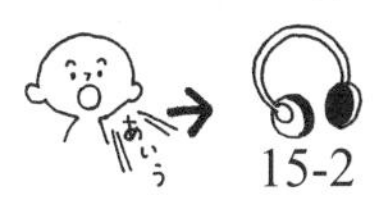

1） ス セ サ ソ シ　ゾ ゼ ジ ザ ズ

2） アジア　サイズ　エンジン

3. Writing Practice

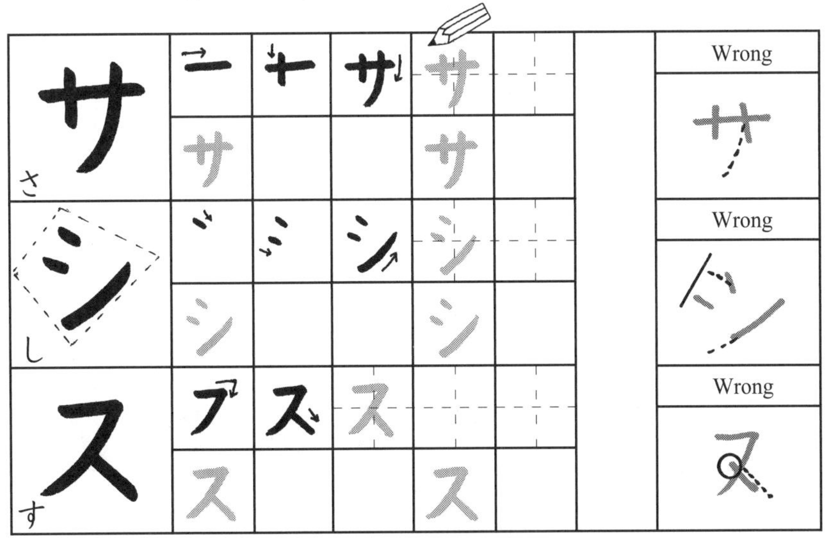

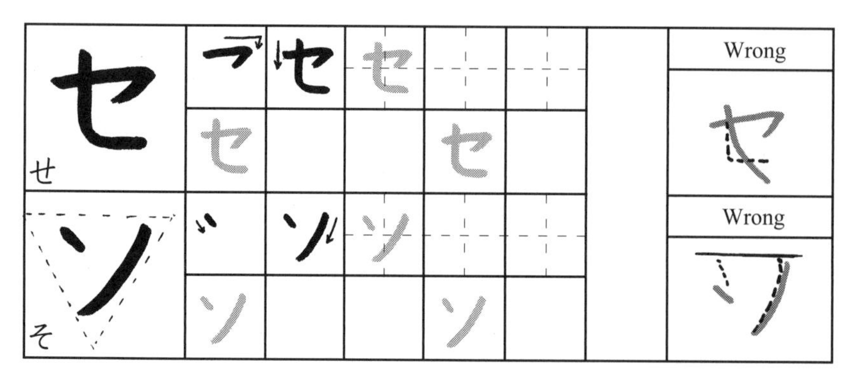

NOTES　How to write ソ

The second stroke starts from the same height as the first one, and comes down from the upper right-hand side to the lower left. Remember to distinguish between ソ and ン when writing.

As shown below, *za*, *ji*, *zu*, *ze* and *zo* are written by adding two dots to サ, シ, ス, セ and ソ.

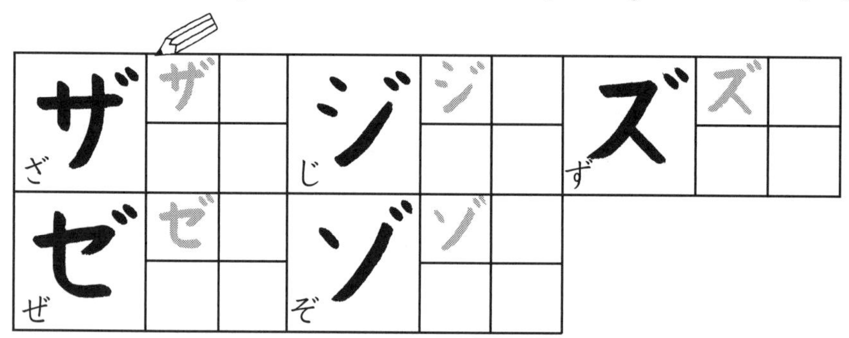

4. Let's write them once again.

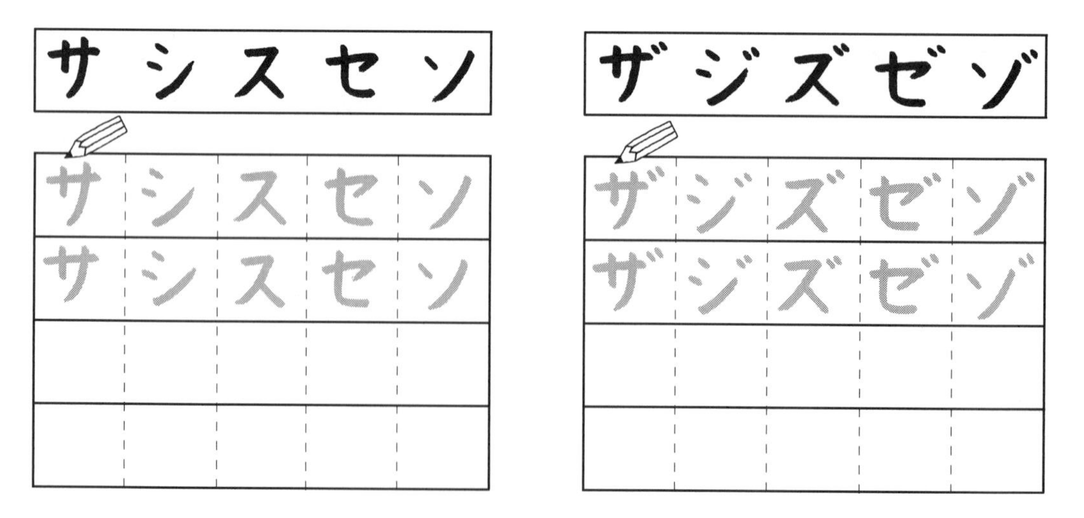

5. Write the katakana letters that correspond to the hiragana letters.

す	ざ	そ	ぜ	さ	す	じ	せ	ぞ	し	ず
ス										

6. Let's write some words!

1） 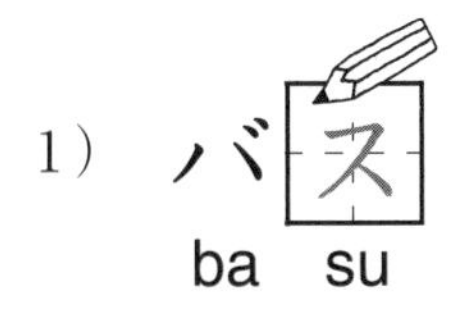 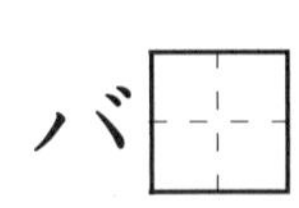 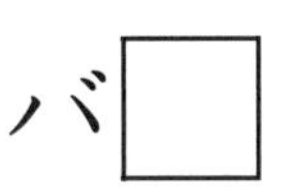

ba su

2） 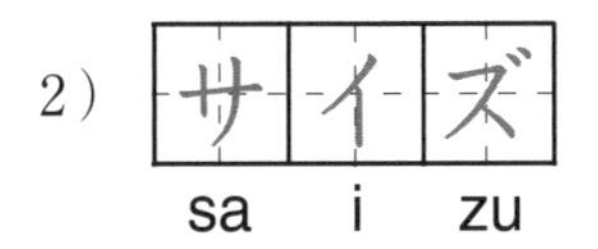 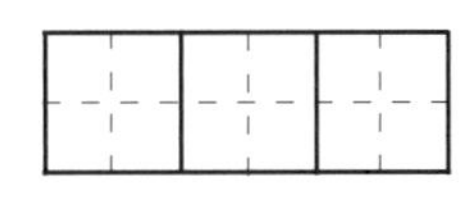 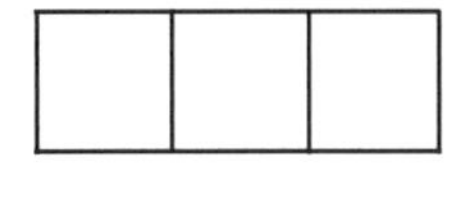

sa i zu

3） ラジカセ 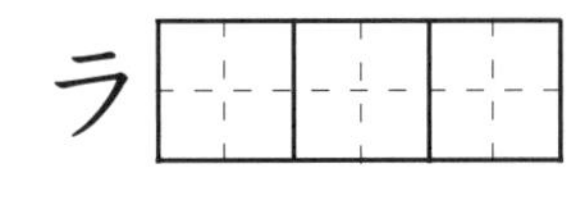 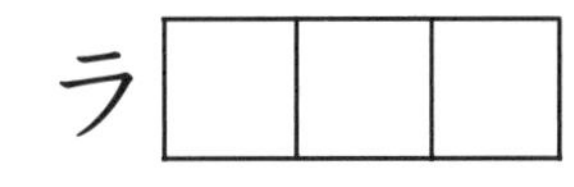

ra ji ka se

4） パソコン パ　　　 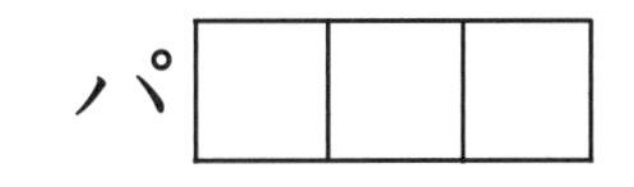

pa so ko n

5） デザイン デ　　　 デ

de za i n

6） マレーシア 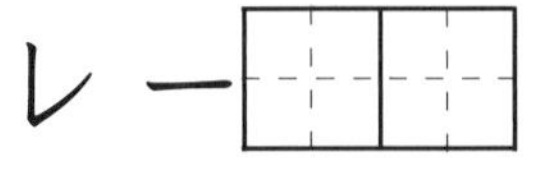

Ma rē shi a

マレー

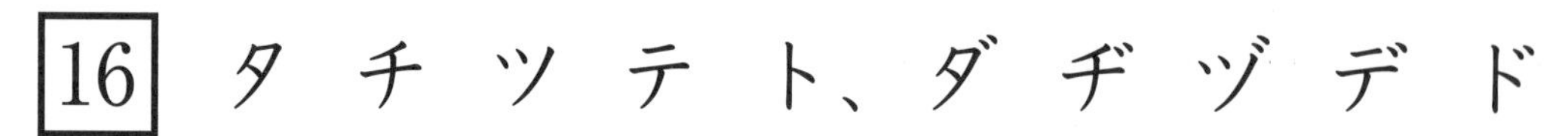

16 タ チ ツ テ ト、ダ ヂ ヅ デ ド

1. Listening Practice

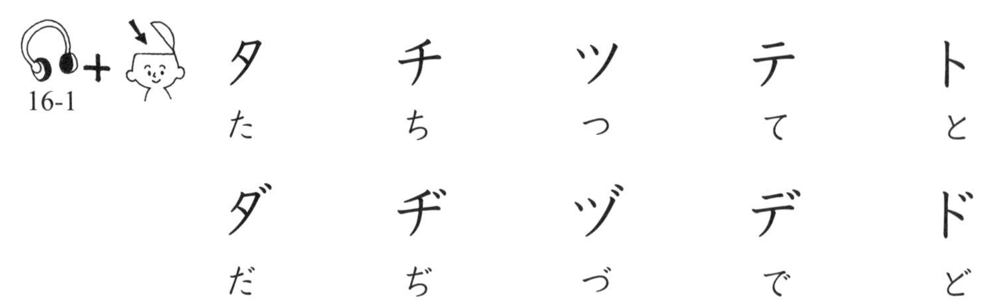

2. Reading Practice

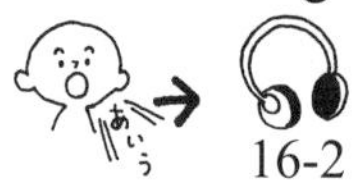

1） チ テ タ ツ ト　デ ダ ヂ ド ヅ

2） タイ　インド　センチ　ダンス　デザイン

3. Writing Practice

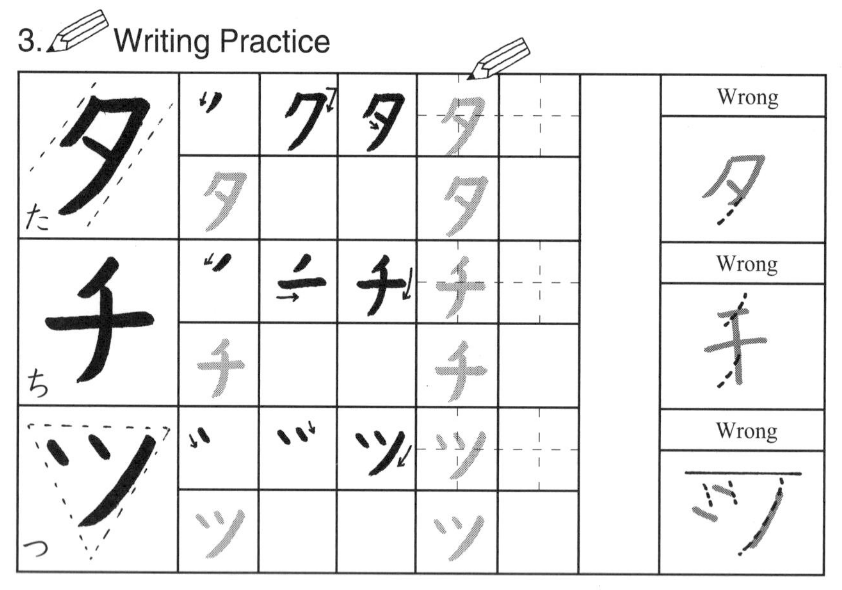

NOTES　How to write ツ

In writing the first and second strokes, write them like two dots put side by side. The third stroke comes down from the upper right-hand side to the lower left. It would be better to write this letter with hiragana つ in mind to distinguish it from シ.

ツ

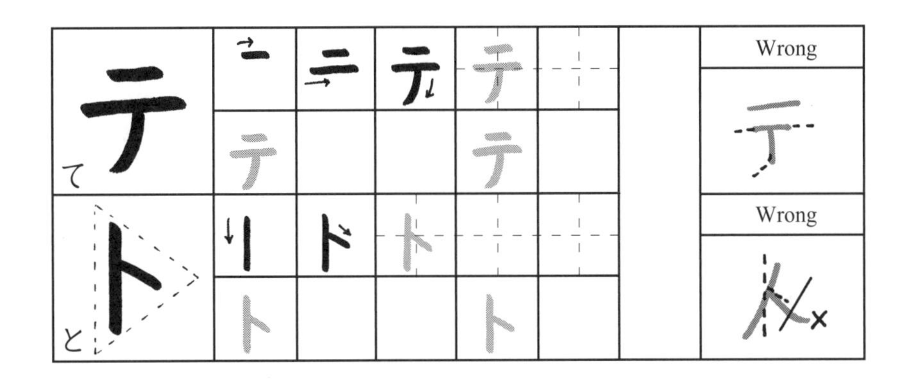

As shown below, *da*, *ji*, *zu*, *de* and *do* are written by adding two dots to タ, チ, ツ, テ and ト.

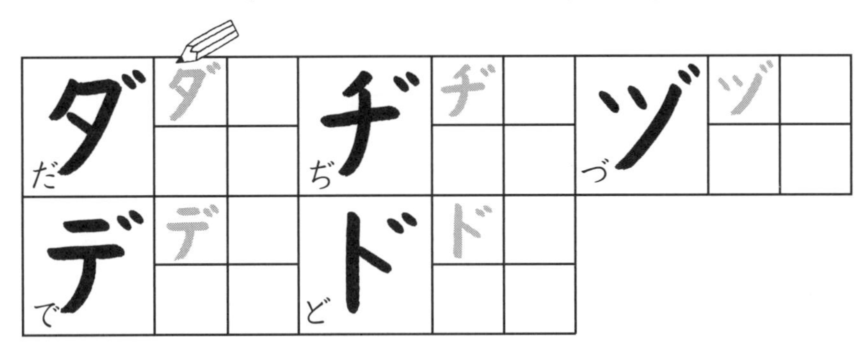

Note that ヂ and ヅ are not generally used.

4. Let's write them once again.

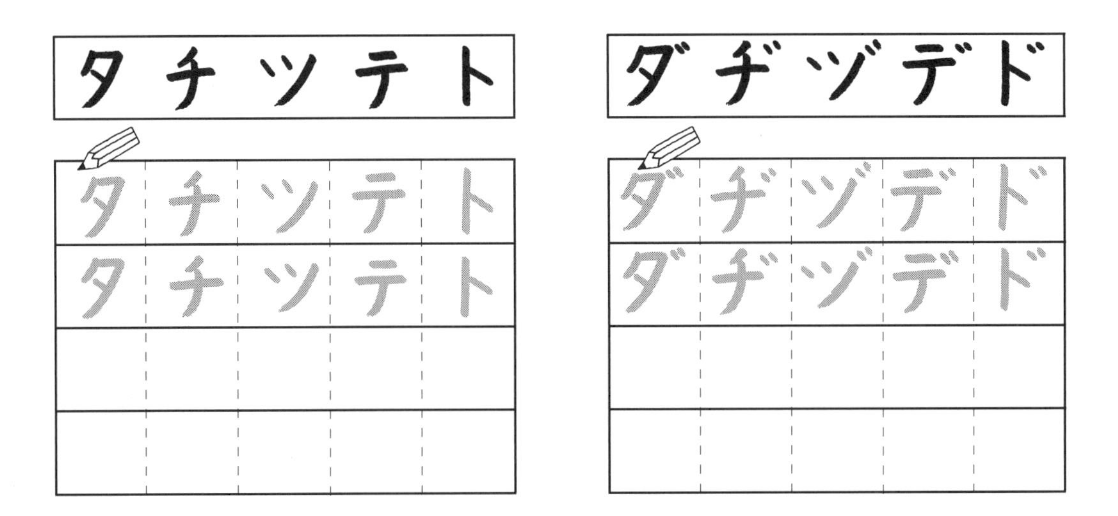

5. Write the katakana letters that correspond to the hiragana letters.

た	づ	ど	ぢ	と	た	で	ち	て	つ	だ
タ										

6. Let's write some words!

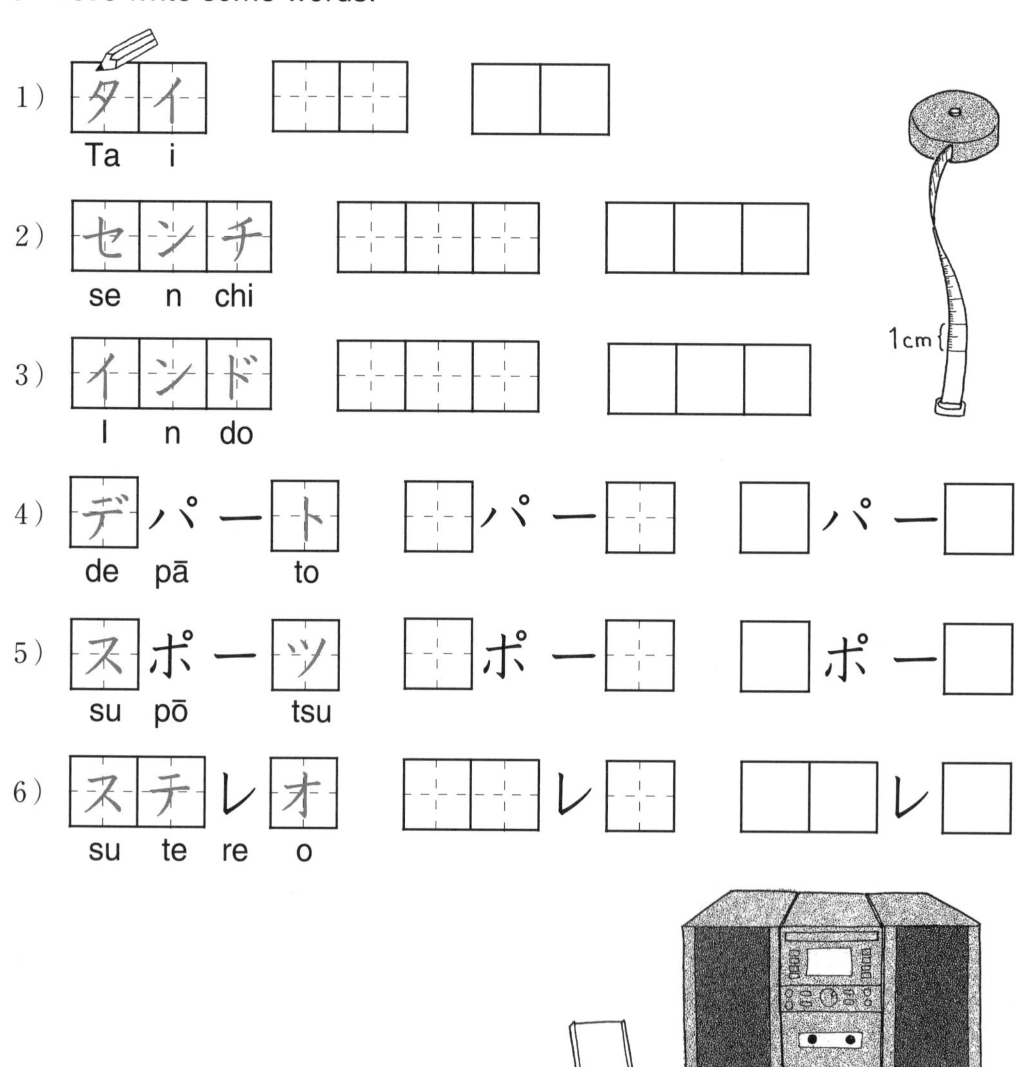

6. 1) Tai (Thailand) 2) senchi (centimeter) 3) Indo (India) 4) depāto (department store)
5) supōtsu (sport) 6) sutereo (stereo)

17 Long Vowels

Long vowels in hiragana are indicated by adding あ, い (え) or う (お) to the previous vowel (see 9, page 37). In the case of katakana, the mark "ー" ("｜" when written vertically) is always used.

1. Listening Practice

17-1

カード	キー	ケーキ	コート
kā do	kii	kē ki	kō to
(card)	(key)	(cake)	(coat)

2. Reading Practice

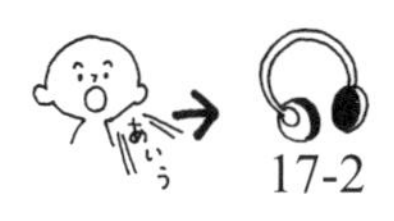

1) ギター　タクシー　センター　スキー
2) コート　カーテン　コンサート　セーター

3. Let's write some words!

1) 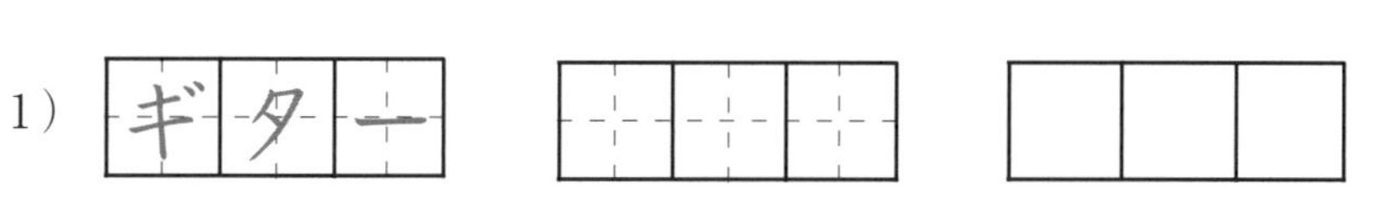

2) 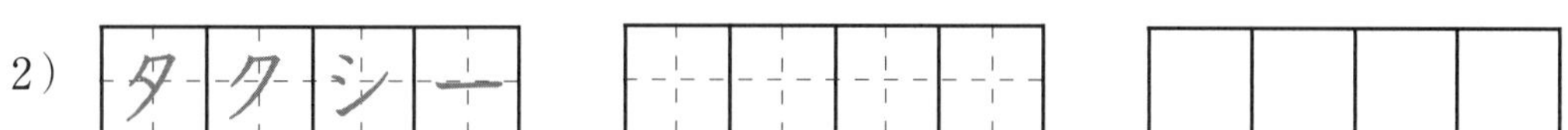

3) 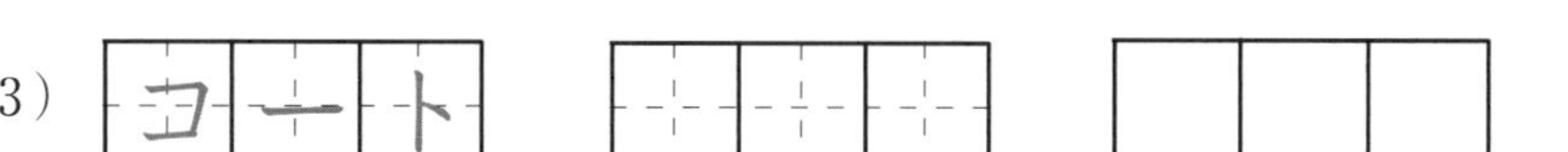

4) 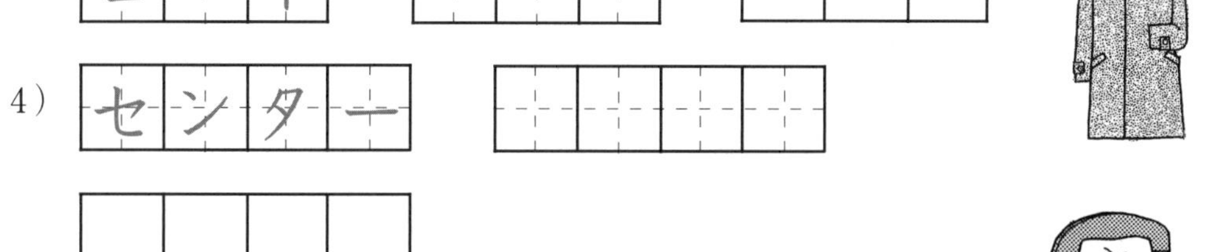

5) シーツ

---

3. 1) gitā (guitar)　2) takushii (taxi)　3) kōto (coat)　4) sentā (center)　5) shiitsu (sheet)

Summary Practice (13 - 17)

1. Reading Practice

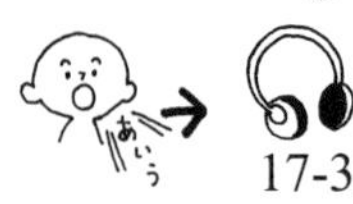

1） ドア　2） ダンス　3） サイズ　4） センチ

5） コート　6） ウイスキー　7） エンジン

2. Writing Practice

Write the katakana letters that correspond to the hiragana letters.

1）

い	と

2）

し	つ

3）

そ	ん

4）

く	た

5）

ち	て

3. Listening and Writing Exercise

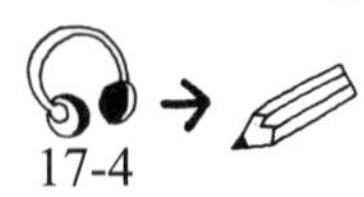

1）

2）

3）

4）

5）

6）

7）

18 ナ　ニ　ヌ　ネ　ノ

1. Listening Practice

18-1

ナ	ニ	ヌ	ネ	ノ
な	に	ぬ	ね	の

2. Reading Practice

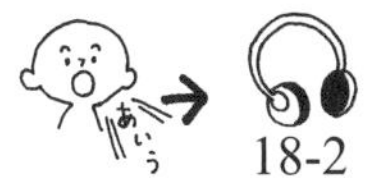

1）ニ　ヌ　ナ　ネ　ノ

2）テニス　ネクタイ　エンジニア　ノート

3. Writing Practice

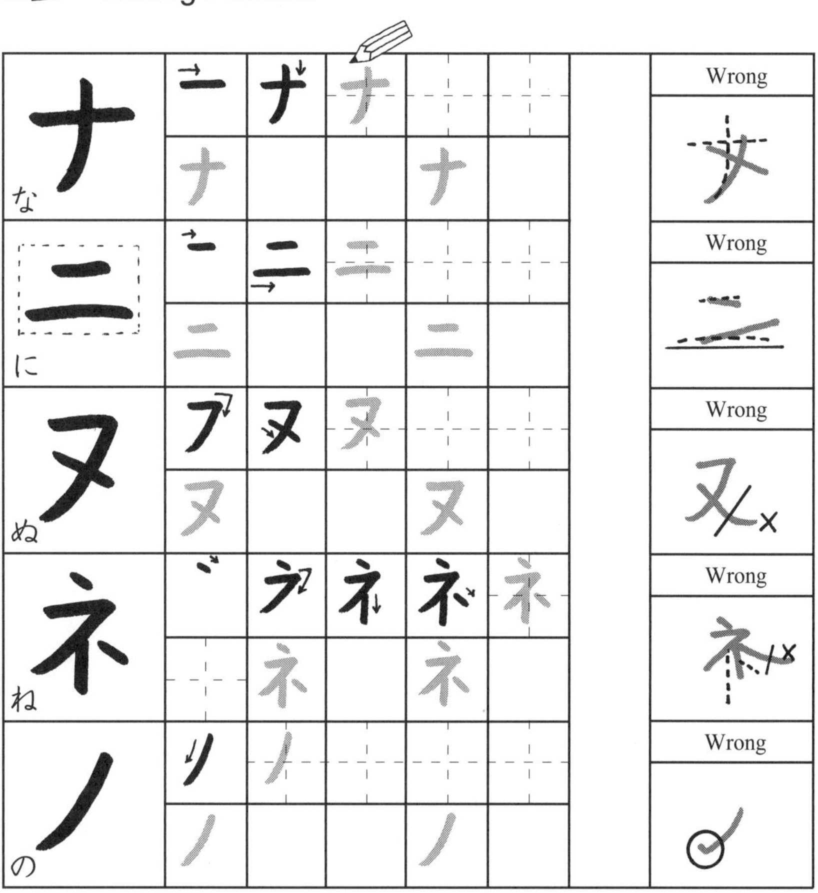

4. Let's write them once again.

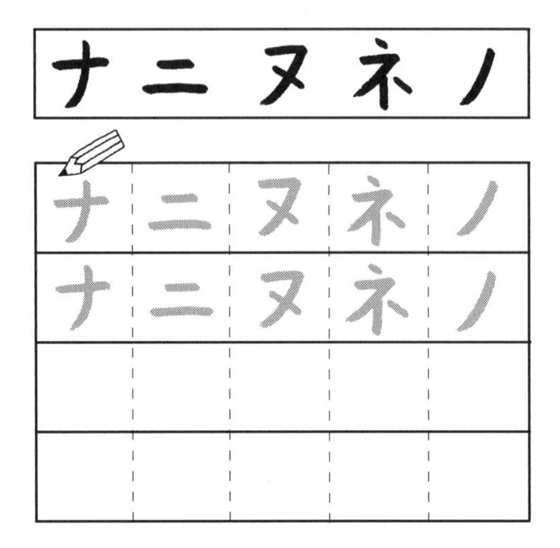

5. Write the katakana letters that correspond to the hiragana letters.

ぬ	の	に	ね	ぬ	な
ヌ					

6. Let's write some words!

1） テニス 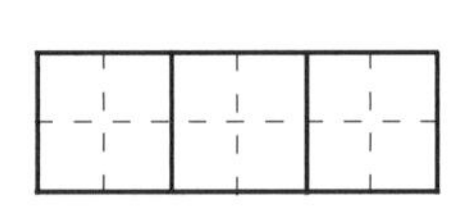 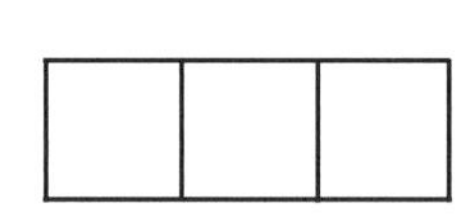 

2） 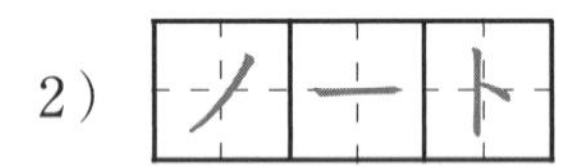

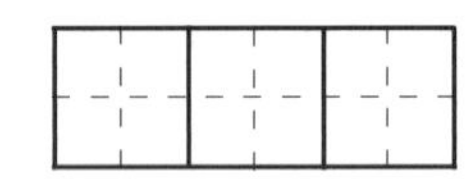 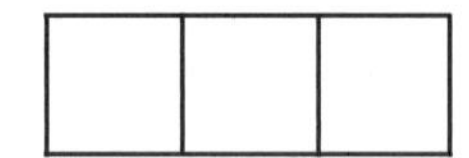 

---

6. 1) tenisu (tennis)　2) nōto (notebook)

6. 3) kanū (canoe) 4) nekutai (necktie) 5) enjinia (engineer) 6) Indoneshia (Indonesia)

19 ハヒフヘホ、バビブベボ、パピプペポ

1. Listening Practice

19-1

ハ	ヒ	フ	ヘ	ホ
は	ひ	ふ	へ	ほ
バ	ビ	ブ	ベ	ボ
ば	び	ぶ	べ	ぼ
パ	ピ	プ	ペ	ポ
ぱ	ぴ	ぷ	ぺ	ぽ

2. Reading Practice

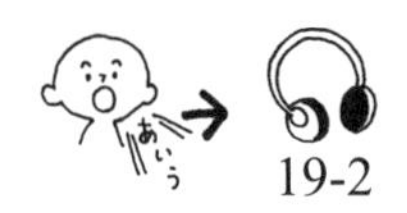

1）ヘ　バ　ポ　フ　ピ　　ボ　ヒ　ベ　ブ　ハ

2）パン　バス　ナイフ　ビデオ　テープ　ピンポン

3. Writing Practice

ハ は	ハ	ハ	ハ				Wrong
	ハ			ハ			
ヒ ひ	ヒ	ヒ	ヒ				Wrong
	ヒ			ヒ			
フ ふ	フ	フ					Wrong
	フ			フ			

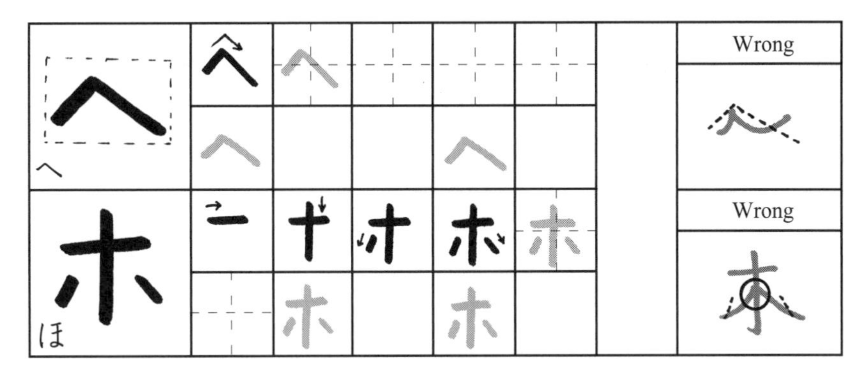

As shown below, *ba*, *bi*, *bu*, *be* and *bo* are written by adding two dots to ハ, ヒ, フ, ヘ and ホ.

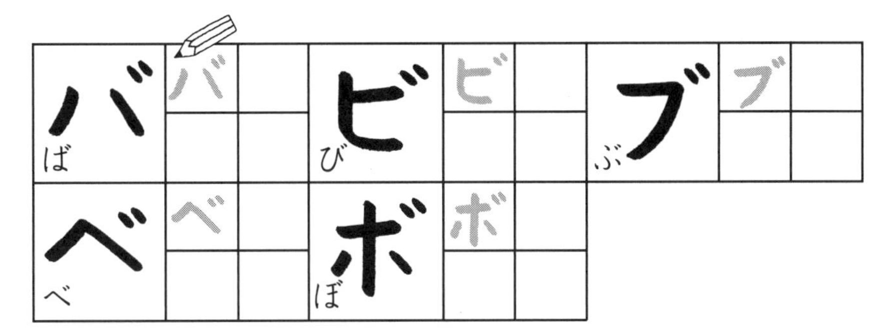

As shown below, *pa*, *pi*, *pu*, *pe* and *po* are written by adding a small circle above the right-hand side of ハ, ヒ, フ, ヘ and ホ.

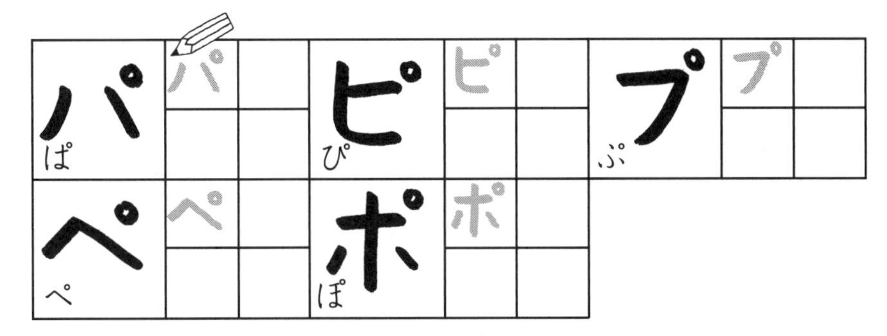

4. Let's write them once again.

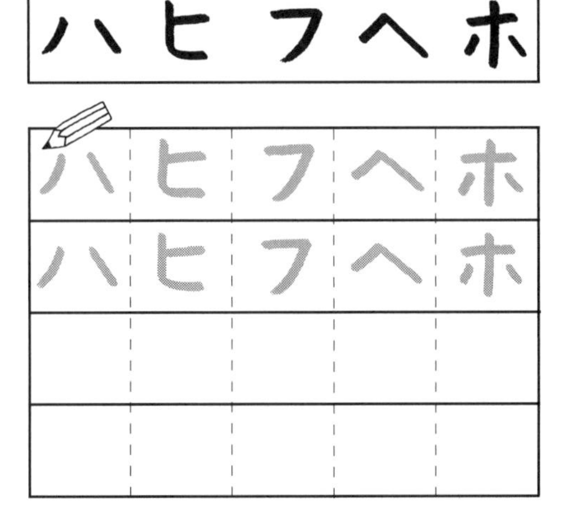

バビブベボ

バビブベボ

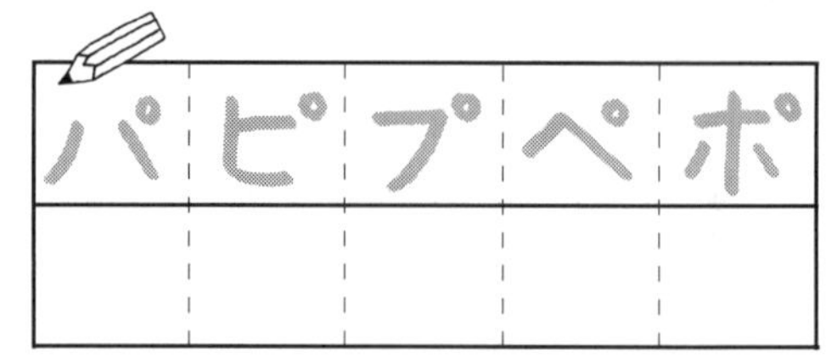

5. Write the katakana letters that correspond to the hiragana letters.

へ	ば	ぼ	ぱ	ぶ	ひ	ぶ	ぺ	は	ぴ	べ	ふ	ぽ	び	ほ
ヘ														

6. Let's write some words!

1) 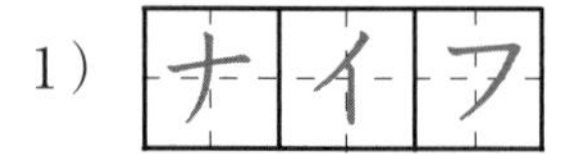 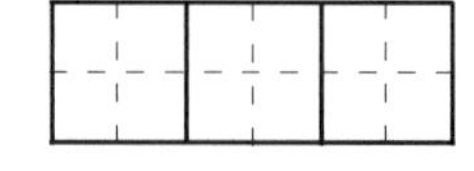 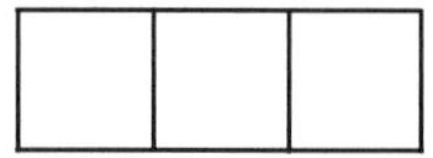 

2) ビデオ 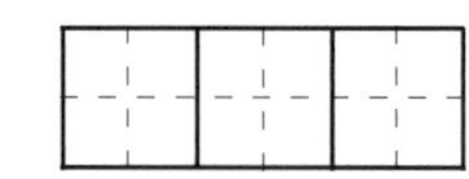 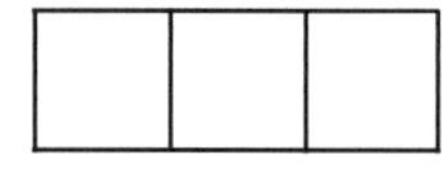

3)  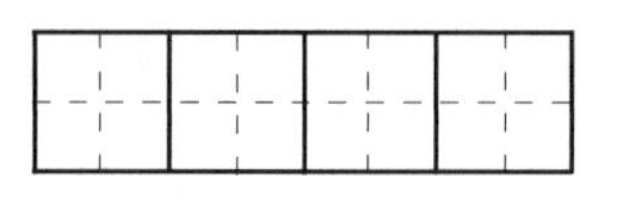 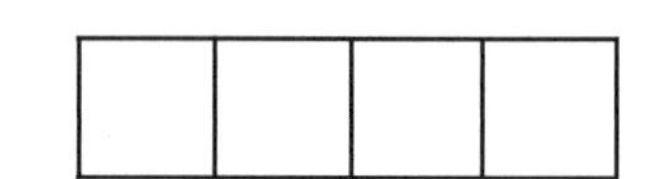

4) 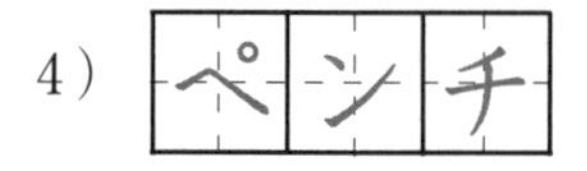 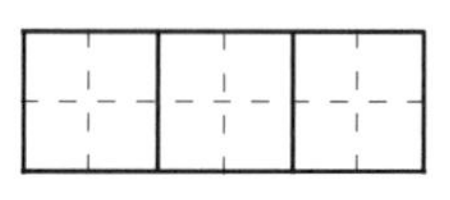 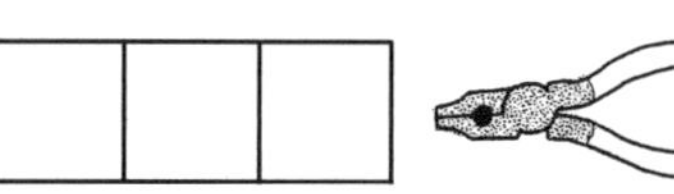

5) 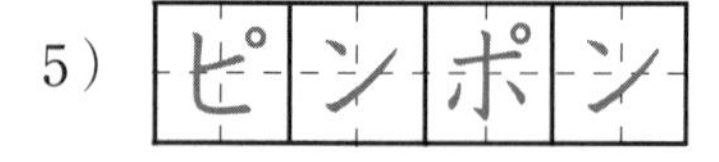 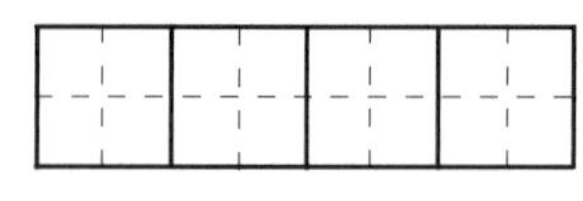 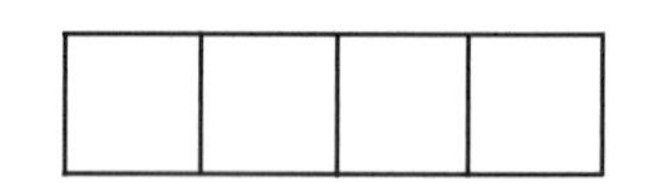

6)  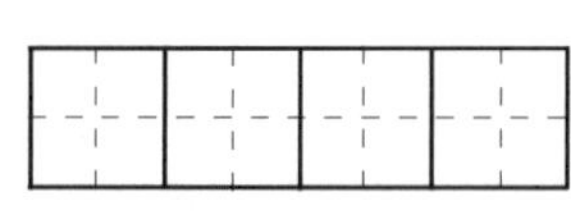 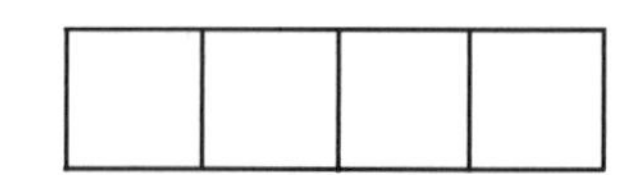

7) 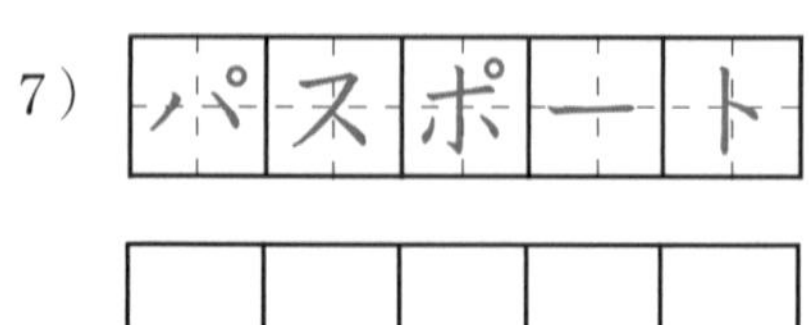 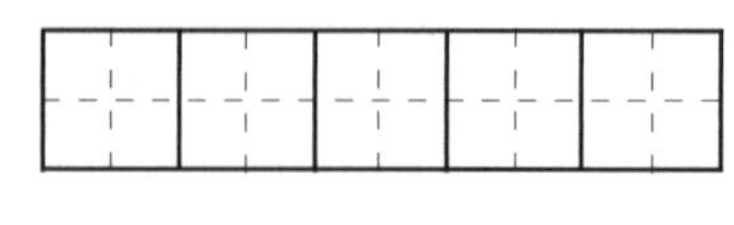 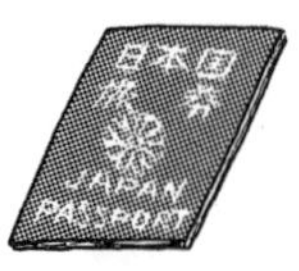

6. 1) naifu (knife) 2) bideo (video) 3) depāto (department store) 4) penchi (cutting pliers) 5) pinpon (table tennis) 6) supūn (spoon) 7) pasupōto (passport)

20 Small Size ッ

Like hiragana (10 , page 40), some katakana words are written using a small ッ.

1. Listening Practice

20-1

コップ	ポケット	サッカー	カセット
ko p pu	po ke t to	sa k kā	ka se t to
(glass)	(pocket)	(soccer)	(cassette)

2. Reading Practice

1）ベッド　コップ　サッカー　ホッチキス

2）カセット　スイッチ　ピクニック

3. Let's write some words!

---

3. 1) koppu (glass [container]) 2) sakkā (soccer) 3) kasetto (cassette) 4) suitchi (switch) 5) pikunikku (picnic)

Summary Practice (18 - 20)

1. Reading Practice

1）テニス　　2）ピアノ　　3）バナナ

4）テープ　　5）エンジニア　　6）ベッド

7）スイッチ　　8）ホッチキス

2. Listening and Writing Exercise

1）				

2）				

3）				

4）				

5）				

6）				

7）				

8）				

21 マ ミ ム メ モ

1. Listening Practice

21-1

マ　　ミ　　ム　　メ　　モ

ま　　み　　む　　め　　も

2. Reading Practice

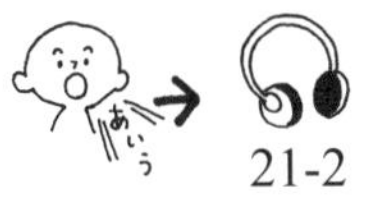

1）ミ　マ　メ　ム　モ

2）メモ　マッチ　ミキサー　ホームステイ

3. Writing Practice

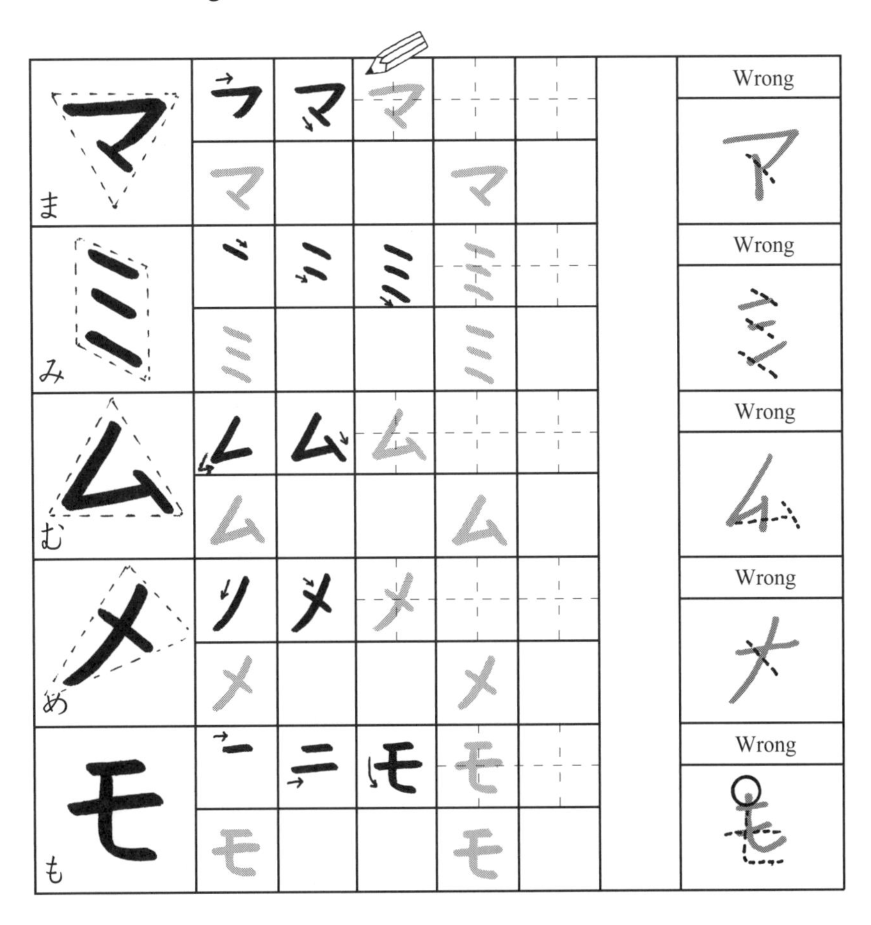

4. Let's write them once again.

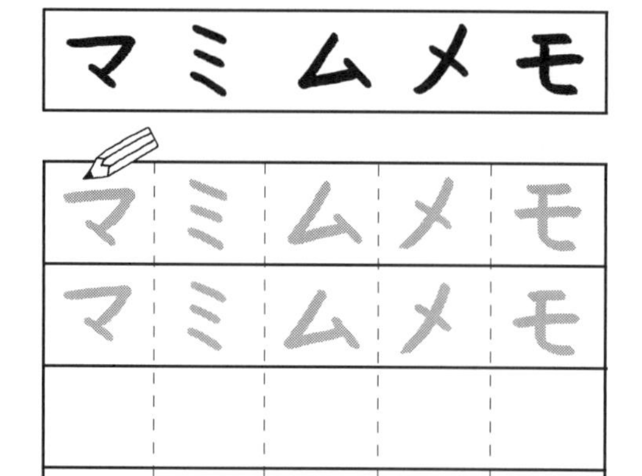

5. Write the katakana letters that correspond to the hiragana letters.

も	み	め	ま	も	む
モ					

6. Let's write some words!

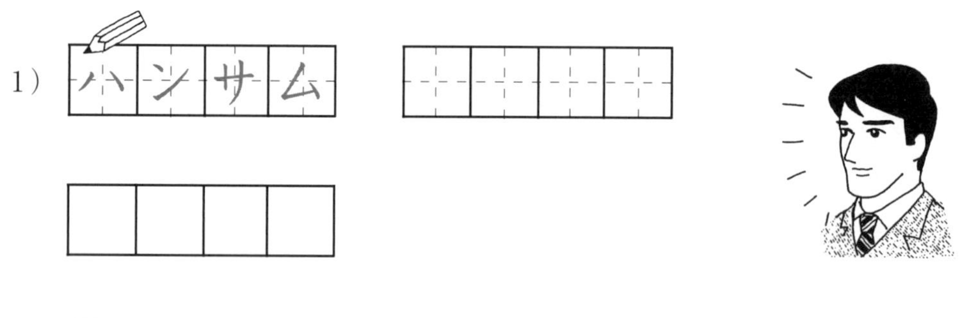

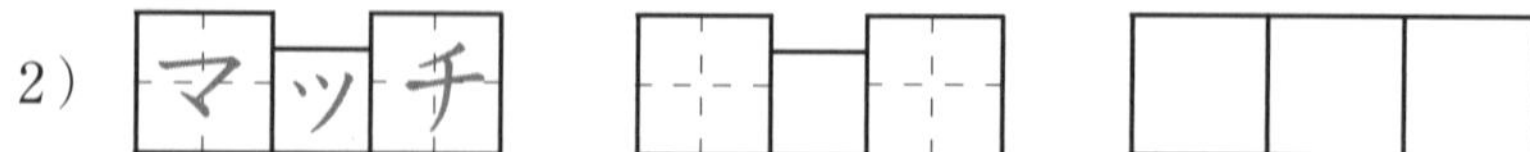

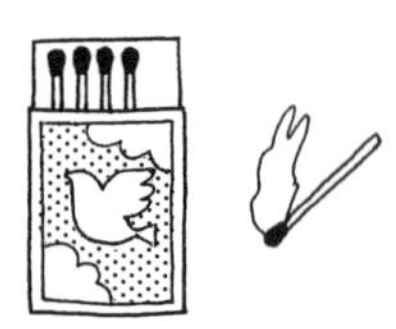

6. 1) hansamu (handsome) 2) matchi (match)

6. 3) mikisā (blender)　4) mēkā (manufacturer)　5) mōtā (motor)　6) hōmusutei (homestay)

22 ラ　リ　ル　レ　ロ

1. Listening Practice

22-1

ラ　リ　ル　レ　ロ
ら　り　る　れ　ろ

2. Reading Practice

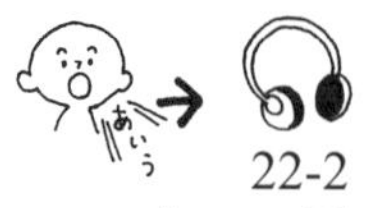

1）ル　ラ　ロ　リ　レ

2）タオル　ライター　アメリカ　ロボット　レストラン

3. Writing Practice

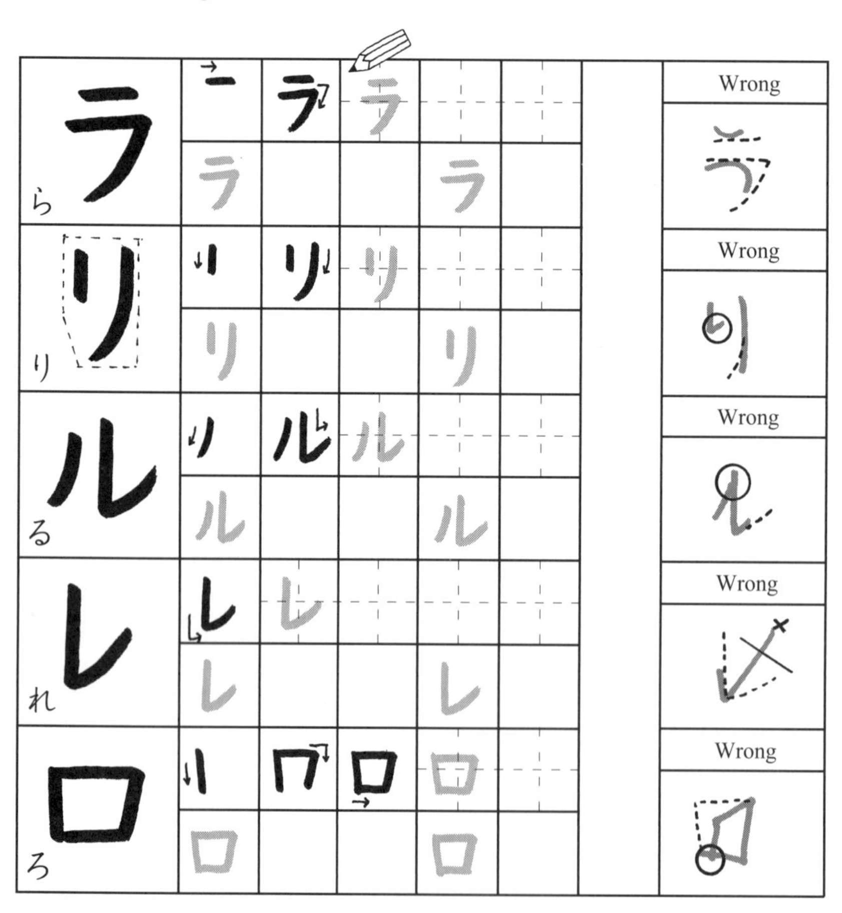

4. Let's write them once again.

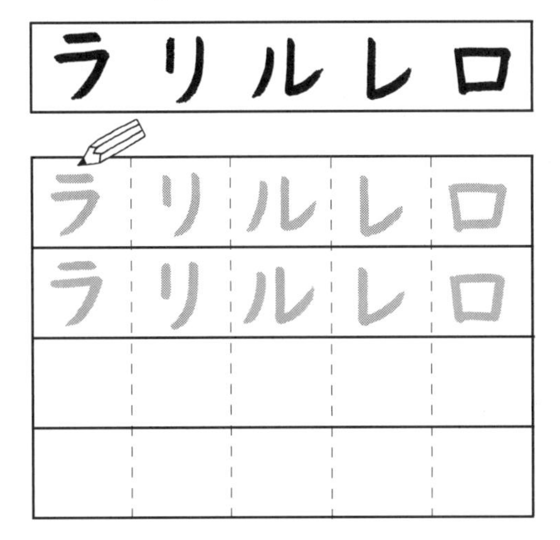

5. Write the katakana letters that correspond to the hiragana letters.

り	れ	ろ	る	ら	り
リ					

6. Let's write some words!

1) ホテル 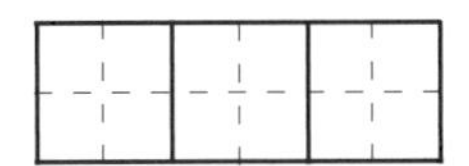 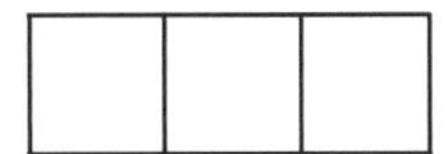

2) アメリカ 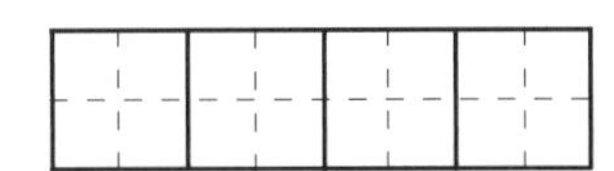 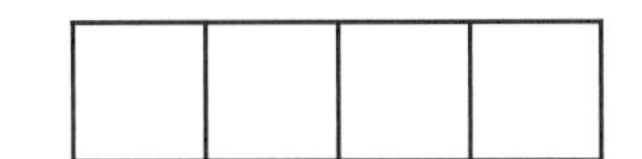

6. 1) hoteru (hotel) 2) Amerika (America)

6. 3) robii (lobby) 4) repōto (report) 5) resutoran (restaurant) 6) raitā (lighter)
7) herumetto (helmet) 8) erebētā (elevator)

23 ヤ　ユ　ヨ、ワ、ヲ

1. Listening Practice

23-1

ヤ　ユ　ヨ
や　ゆ　よ

ワ　ヲ
わ　を

2. Reading Practice

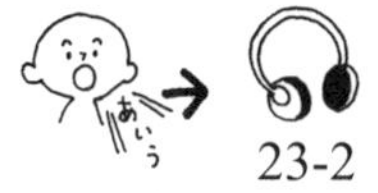

1）ヤ　ユ　ワ　ヨ　ユ

2）タワー　タイヤ　ワープロ　ヨーロッパ

3. Writing Practice

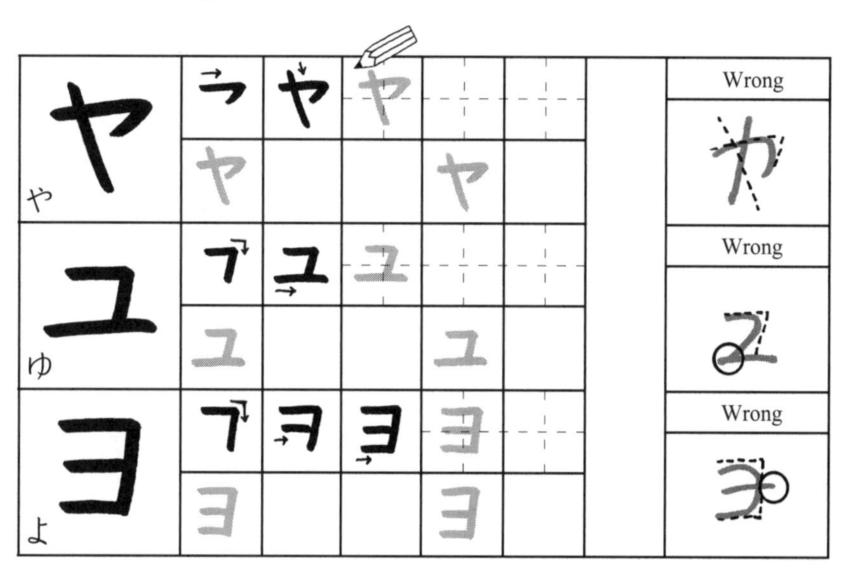

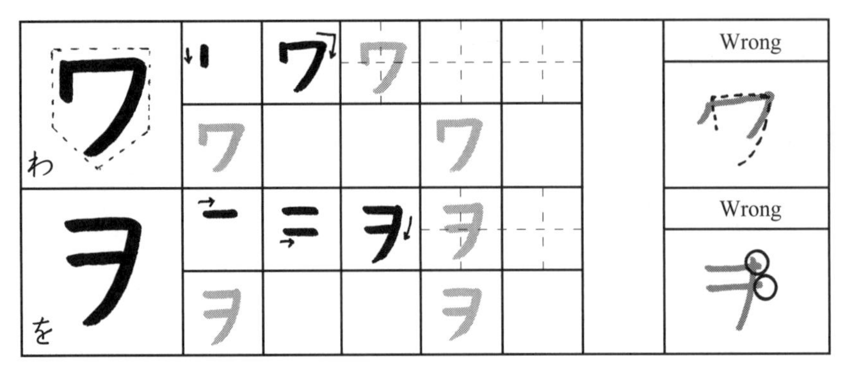

Note that ヲ is not generally used.

4. Let's write them once again.

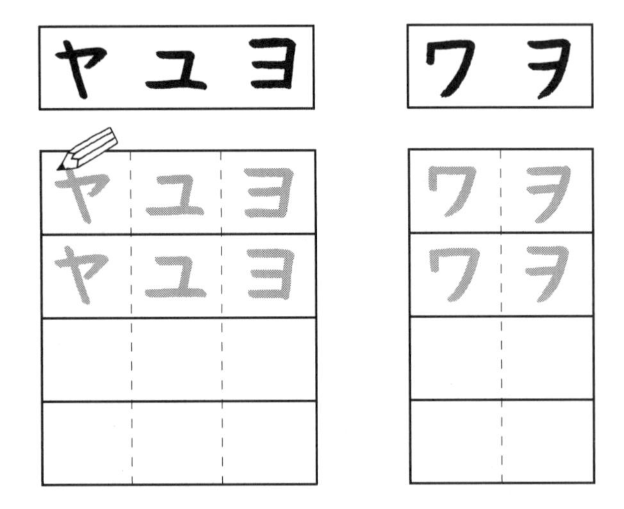

5. Write the katakana letters that correspond to the hiragana letters.

を	や	わ	よ	ゆ
ヲ				

6. Let’s write some words!

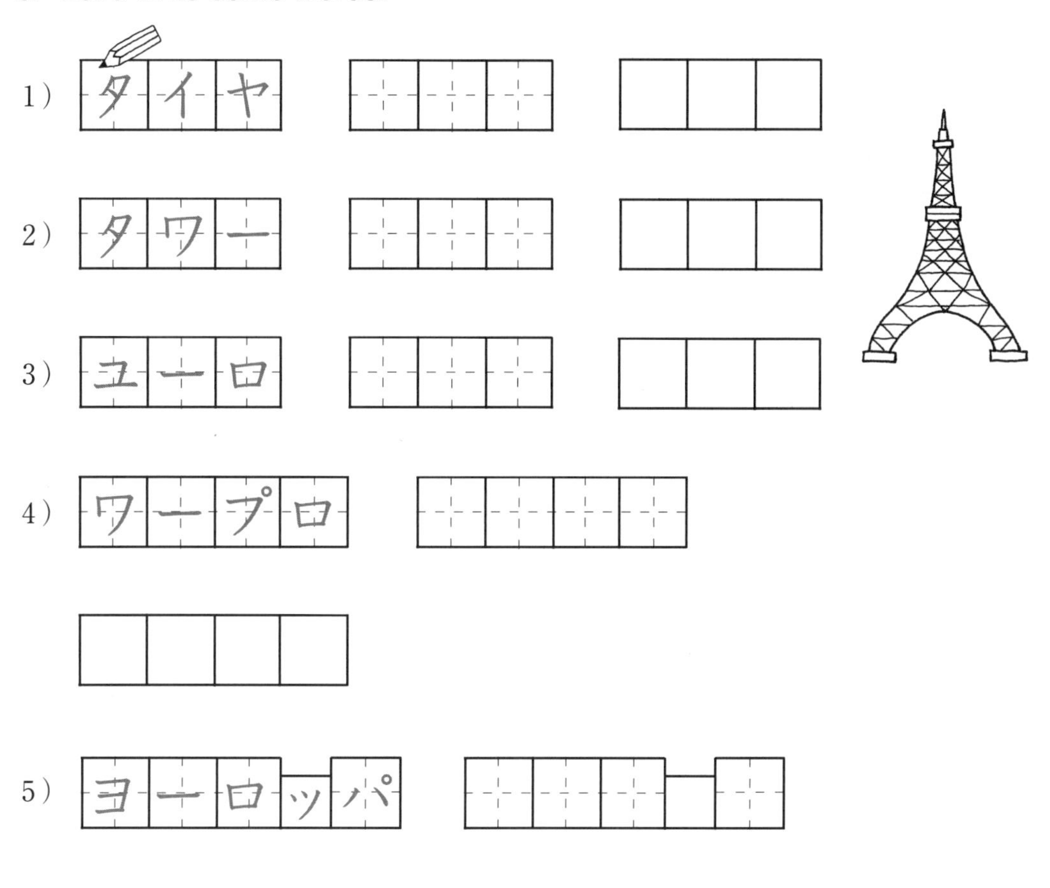

5) ヨーロッパ

6)

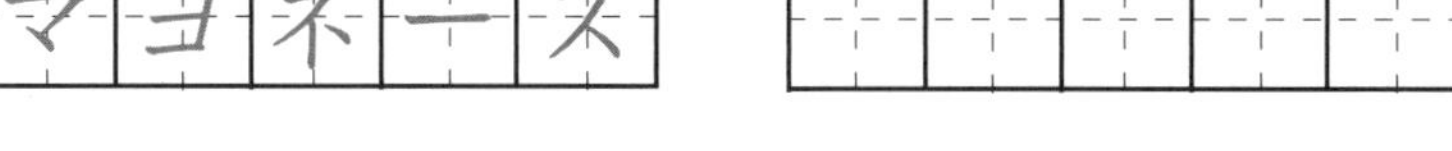

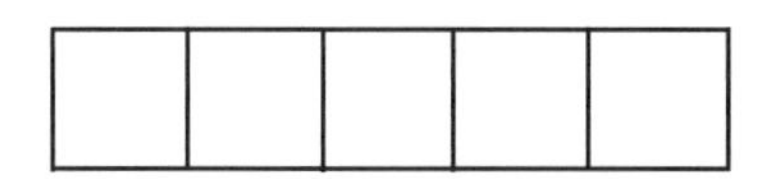

6. 1) taiya (tyre) 2) tawā (tower) 3) Yūro (Euro) 4) wāpuro (word processor)
5) Yōroppa (Europe) 6) mayonēzu (mayonnaise)

Let's Check!

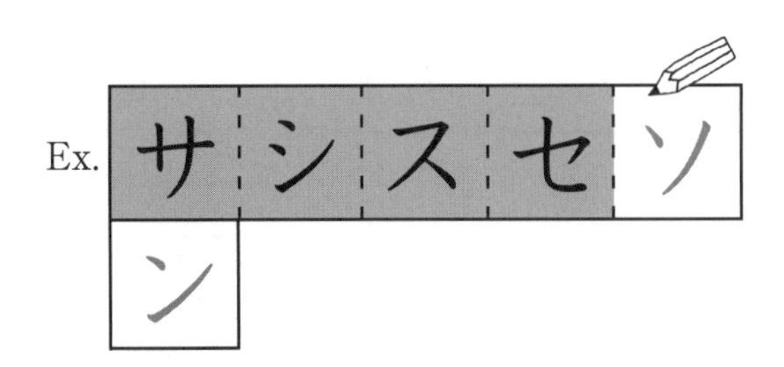

1)

サ	1	ス	セ	ソ
タ	チ	2	テ	ト

2)

3	イ	ウ	エ	オ
4	ミ	ム	メ	モ

3)

5	ニ	ヌ	ネ	ノ
マ	ミ	ム	6	モ

4)

サ	シ	7	セ	ソ
ナ	ニ	8	ネ	ノ

5)

タ	9	ツ	10	ト

6)

ア	11	ウ	エ	オ
タ	チ	ツ	テ	12

7)

サ	シ	ス	13	ソ
14		ユ		ヨ

8)

カ	キ	ク	ケ	15
ヤ		16		ヨ

9)

カ	キ	17	18	コ
19				ヲ

Test 4

Complete the katakana list.

あ ア	い	う	え	お
か	き	く	け	こ
さ	し	す	せ	そ
た	ち	つ	て	と
な	に	ぬ	ね	の
は	ひ	ふ	へ	ほ
ま	み	む	め	も
や		ゆ		よ
ら	り	る	れ	ろ
わ				を ヲ
ん				

Test 5

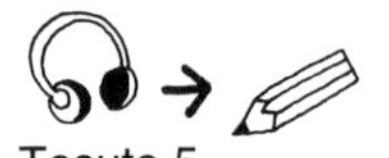

Tesuto 5

Listen to the CD and write the katakana letters in the boxes.

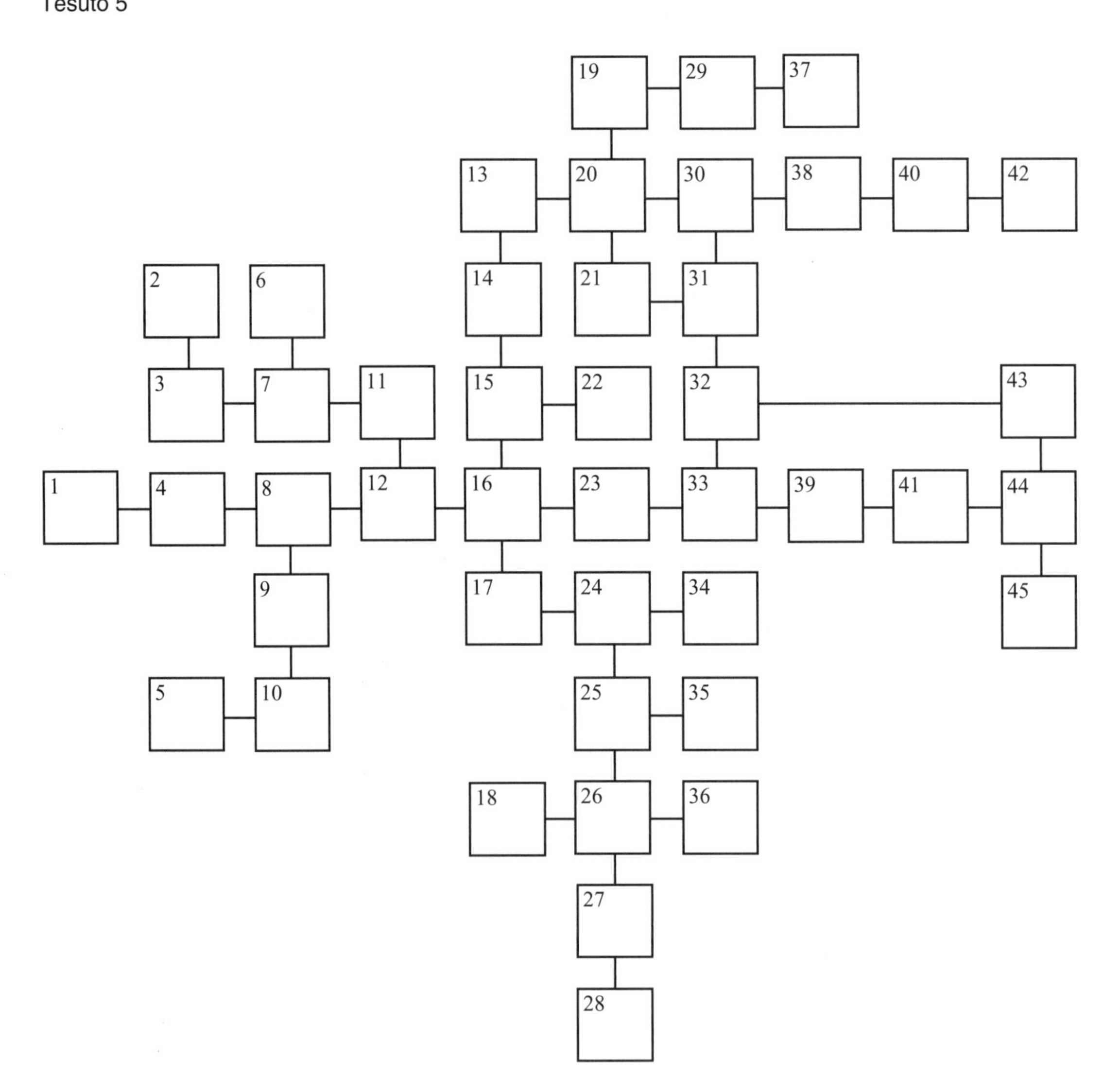

24　キャ、キュ、キョ

As you learnt in 11 (page 42), the combination of a normal-sized letter and a small-sized ャ, ュ or ョ is read as one syllable.

1. Listening Practice

24-1

シャツ	ジュース	アクション
sha tsu	jū su	a ku sho n
(shirt)	(juice)	(action)

2. Reading Practice

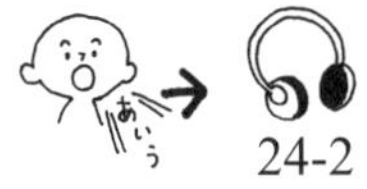

1）シャツ　シャワー　シャープペンシル

2）ジュース　ニュース　スケジュール
　　コンピューター　ジョギング

3. Writing Practice

As with a small ッ, when ○ャ, ○ュ or ○ョ is written, it should be written at the lower left-hand side at half the normal size.

Ex.

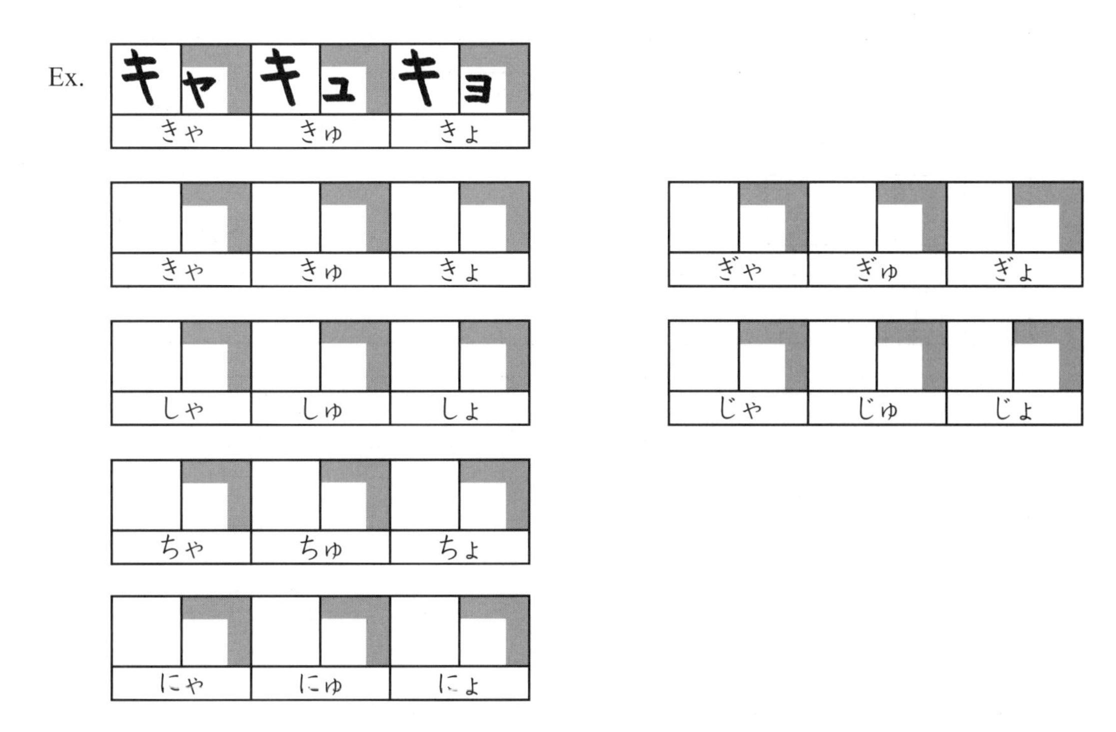

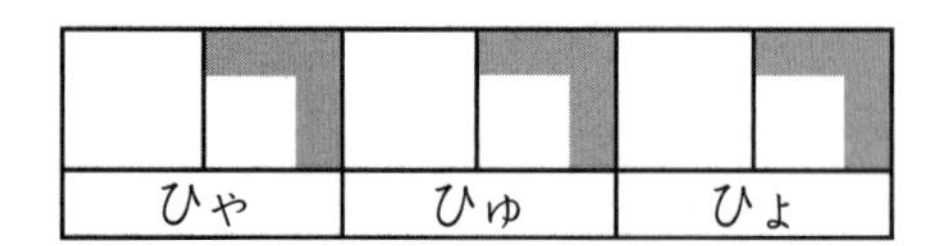

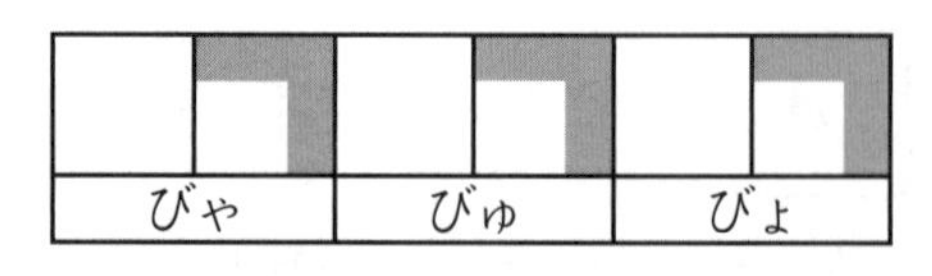

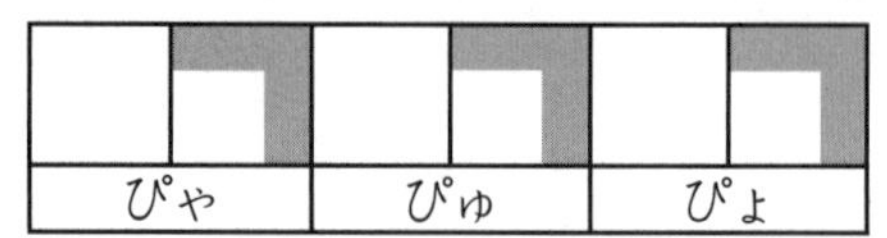

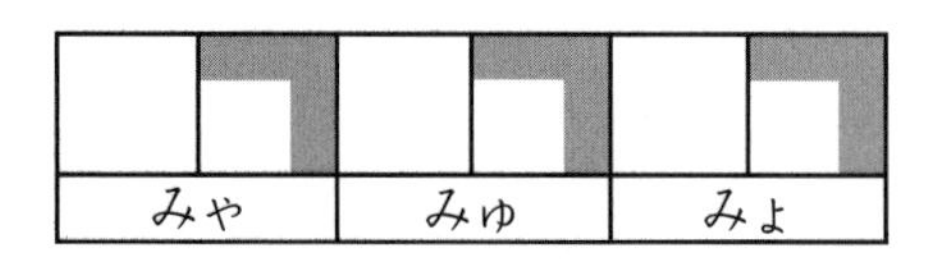

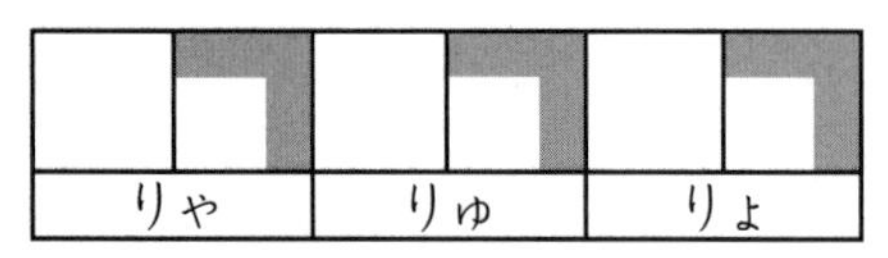

4. Let's write some words!

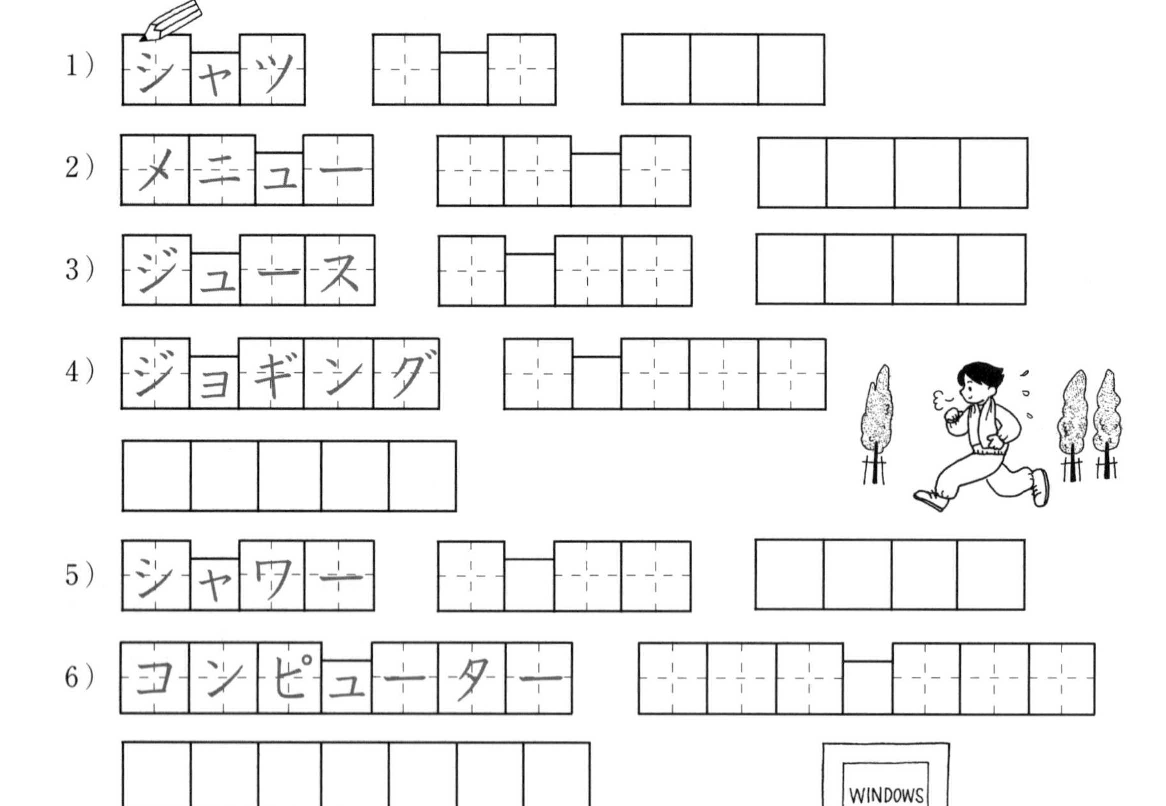

4. 1) shatsu (shirt) 2) menyū (menu) 3) jūsu (juice) 4) jogingu (jogging)
5) shawā (shower) 6) konpyūtā (computer)

Summary Practice (21 - 24)

1. Reading Practice

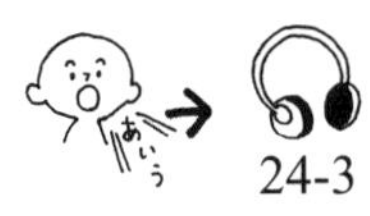

1） ゴム　　2） ミルク　　3） ラジカセ

4） マレーシア　　5） シャツ　　6） コンピューター

7） ジョギング

2. Listening and Writing Exercise

1） 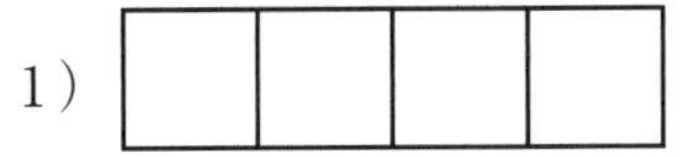

2）

3）

4）

5）

6）

7）

25 Small Size ァ・ィ・ゥ・ェ・ォ

1. Listening Practice

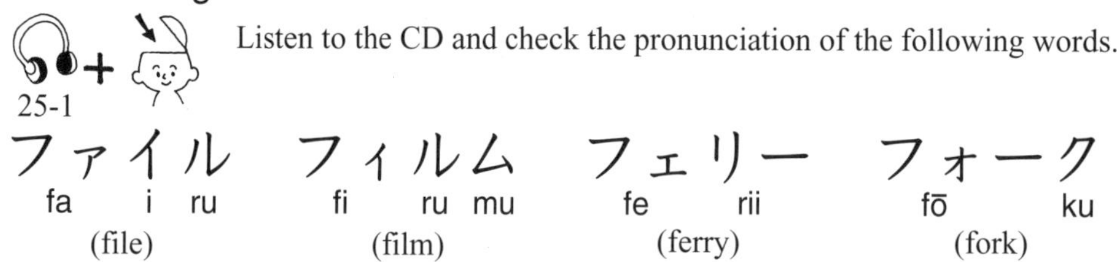

Listen to the CD and check the pronunciation of the following words.

ファイル (fa i ru) (file)　フィルム (fi ru mu) (film)　フェリー (fe rii) (ferry)　フォーク (fō ku) (fork)

In order to write foreign words, the combination of katakana letters may be written like below, a style not used in hiragana. Each example represents the combination of a normal-sized letter with a small-sized ァ, ィ, ゥ, ェ or ォ, with each combination representing one syllable. Though ゥ is rarely used, it is when writing トゥ and ドゥ.

Check the pronunciation and how these sounds are written while listening to the CD.

25-2

	ウィ wi		ウェ we	ウォ wo
クァ kwa	クィ kwi		クェ kwe	クォ kwo
グァ gwa				
			シェ she	
			チェ che	
	ティ ti			
	ディ di			
		トゥ tu		
		ドゥ du		
ファ fa	フィ fi		フェ fe	フォ fo

NOTES

Beside the examples in the table, other combinations may be used in order to make the sound as close as possible to the original sound of a foreign word or the name of a foreign place.

Ex. ヴィエトナム (Vietnam)
　　フィレンツェ (Firenze, Florence)

There are some other words using a small-sized ュ other than the combinations which you have learned in the table in chapter 24 on pages 93 and 94.

Ex. プロデューサー (producer)

2. Reading Practice

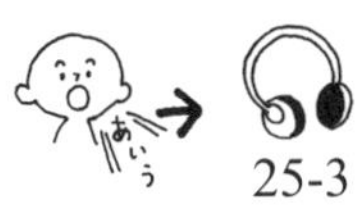

1）ファックス　　2）フィリピン　3）ボディー

4）ミーティング　5）チェック　　6）フォーク

3. Let's write some words!

4）ファックス

5）フォーク

6）チェック

3. 1) firumu (film)　2) disuko (disco)　3) pātii (party)　4) fakkusu (facsimile)　5) fōku (fork)　6) chekku (check)

Vertical Writing

Horizontally written ①サッカー, ②ジュース and ③フォーク will become ④, ⑤ and ⑥ when written vertically. Small letters such as ッ and ォ should be written at the upper right-hand side. As was explained in 17, the long vowel mark "ー" is indicated with a vertical line, "丨", when written vertically.

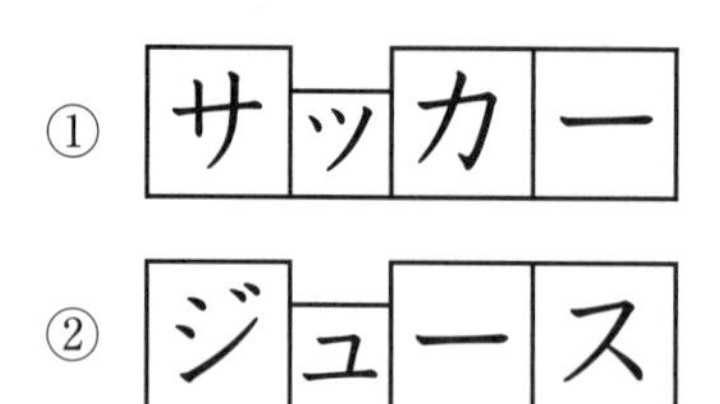

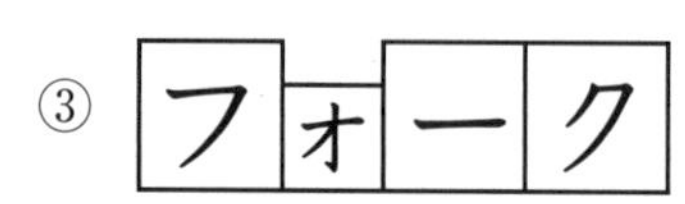

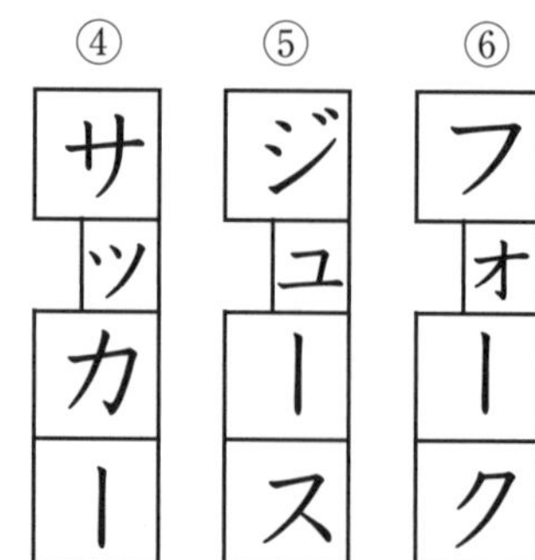

1. Reading Practice

Read the names of the cities from ① to ⑭ shown below.

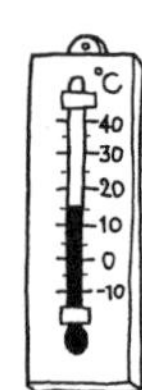

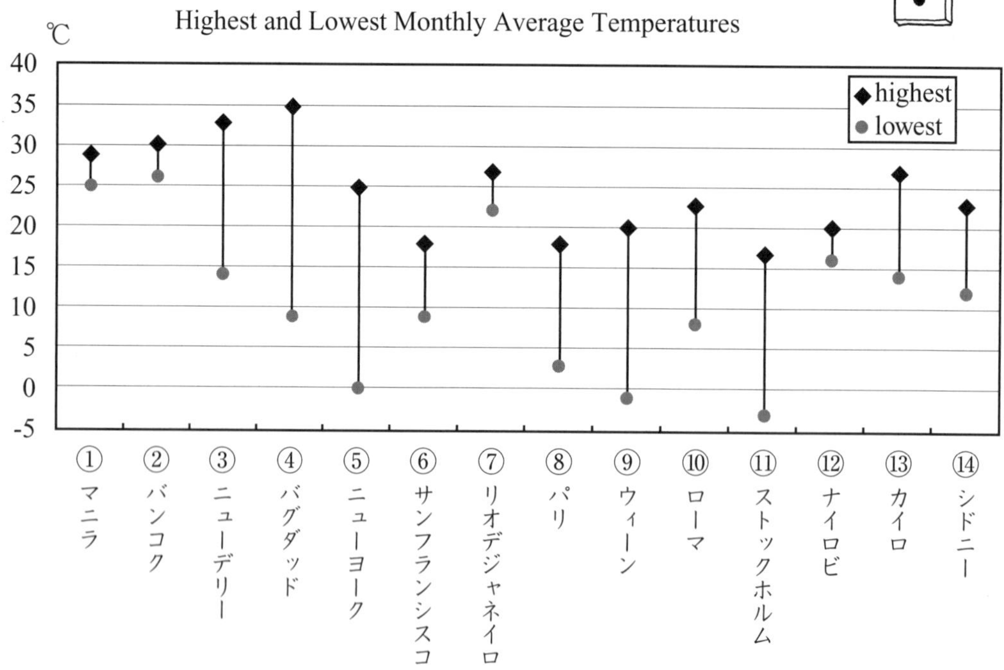

---

1. ① Manira (Manila) ② Bankoku (Bangkok)
③ Nyūderii (New Delhi) ④ Bagudaddo (Baghdad)
⑤ Nyūyōku (New York) ⑥ Sanfuranshisuko (San Francisco)
⑦ Riodejaneiro (Rio de Janeiro) ⑧ Pari (Paris)
⑨ Wiin (Wien, Vienna) ⑩ Rōma (Rome)
⑪ Sutokkuhorumu (Stockholm) ⑫ Nairobi (Nairobi)
⑬ Kairo (Cairo) ⑭ Shidonii (Sydney)

Crossword Puzzles

1)

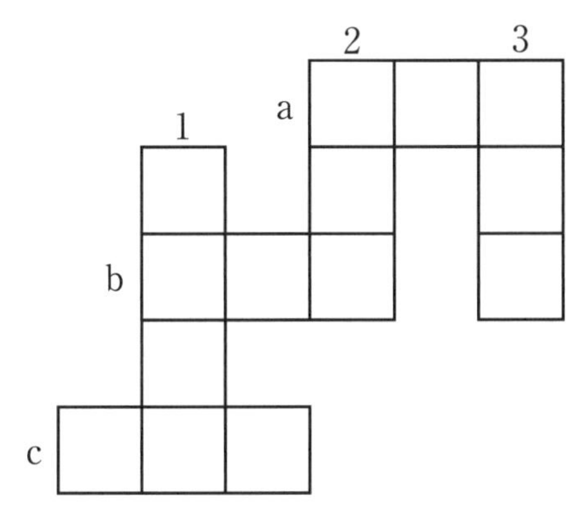

Down
1 necktie
2 tennis
3 video

Across
a television
b class
c typewriter

2)

Down
1 bread
2 India
3 America
4 stereo

Across
a England
b table tennis
c door
d camera

Test 6

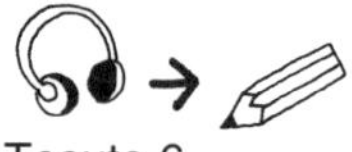

Tesuto 6

Listen to the CD and write down the words in katakana in the boxes.

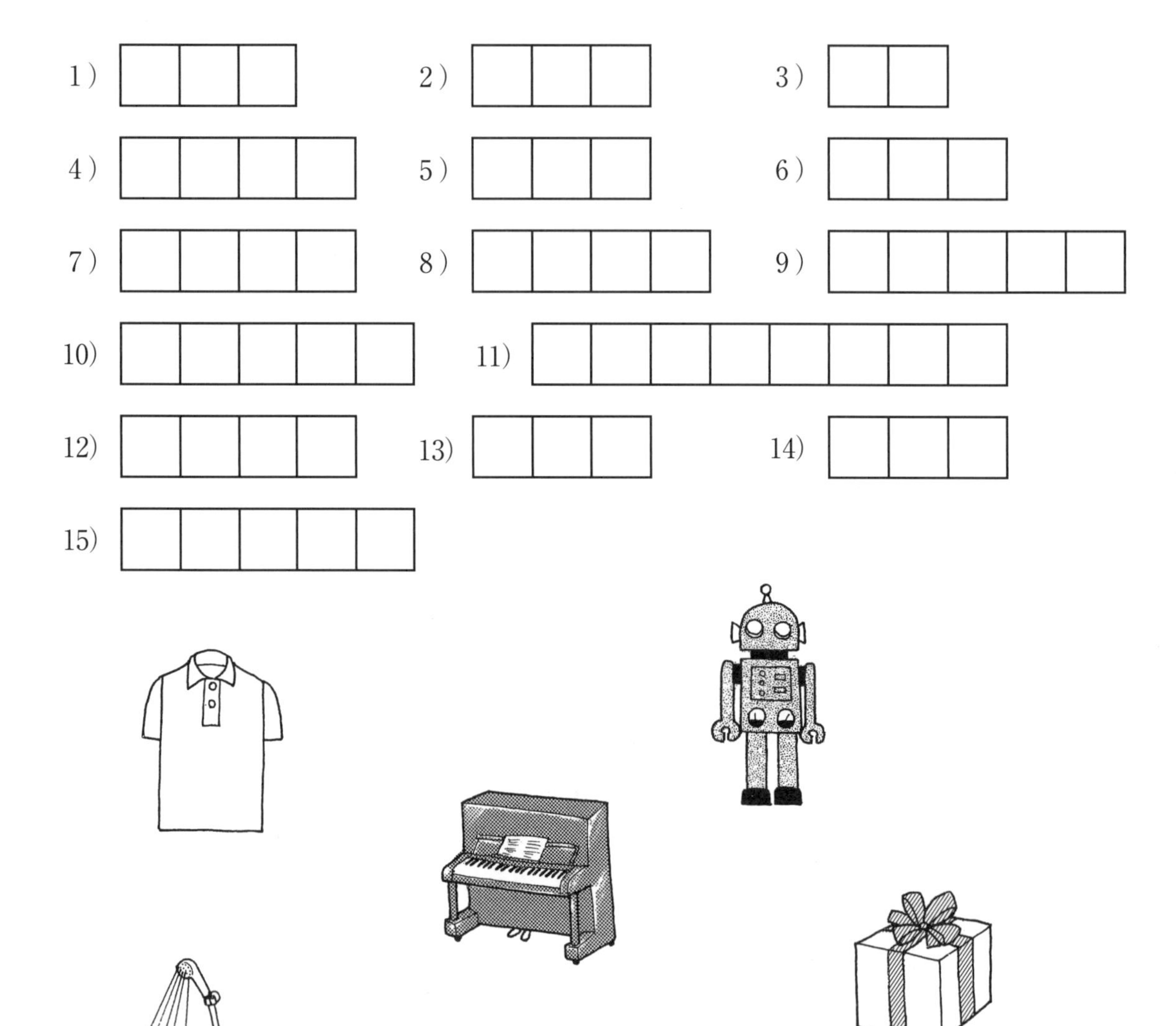

Summary Quiz (1)

What are the cities of the following countries? Choose the correct ones from a to p in the square below.

Ex. フィリピン	(m)	1. ベトナム	( )
2. タイ	( )	3. マレーシア	( )
4. インドネシア	( )	5. インド	( )
6. スリランカ	( )	7. パキスタン	( )
8. エジプト	( )	9. イギリス	( )
10. フランス	( )	11. ドイツ	( )
12. スペイン	( )	13. イタリア	( )
14. アメリカ	( )	15. ブラジル	( )

a	b	c	d	e	f	g	h	i	j	k	l	m	n	o	p
イスラマバード	カイロ	クアラルンプール	コロンボ	ジャカルタ	ニューデリー	ハノイ	バンコク	パリ	ブラジリア	ベルリン	マドリード	マニラ	ローマ	ロンドン	ワシントン

Ex. Philippines 1. Vietnam 2. Thailand 3. Malaysia 4. Indonesia 5. India 6. Sri Lanka 7. Pakistan 8. Egypt 9. United Kingdom 10. France 11. Germany 12. Spain 13. Italy 14. U.S.A. 15. Brazil

a. Islamabad b. Cairo c. Kuala Lumpur d. Colombo e. Jakarta f. New Delhi g. Hanoi h. Bangkok i. Paris j. Brazilia k. Berlin l. Madrid m. Manila n. Rome o. London p. Washington, D.C.

Summary Quiz (2)

Write the names of the countries in the boxes in katakana by referring to the names written in *Romaji* below.

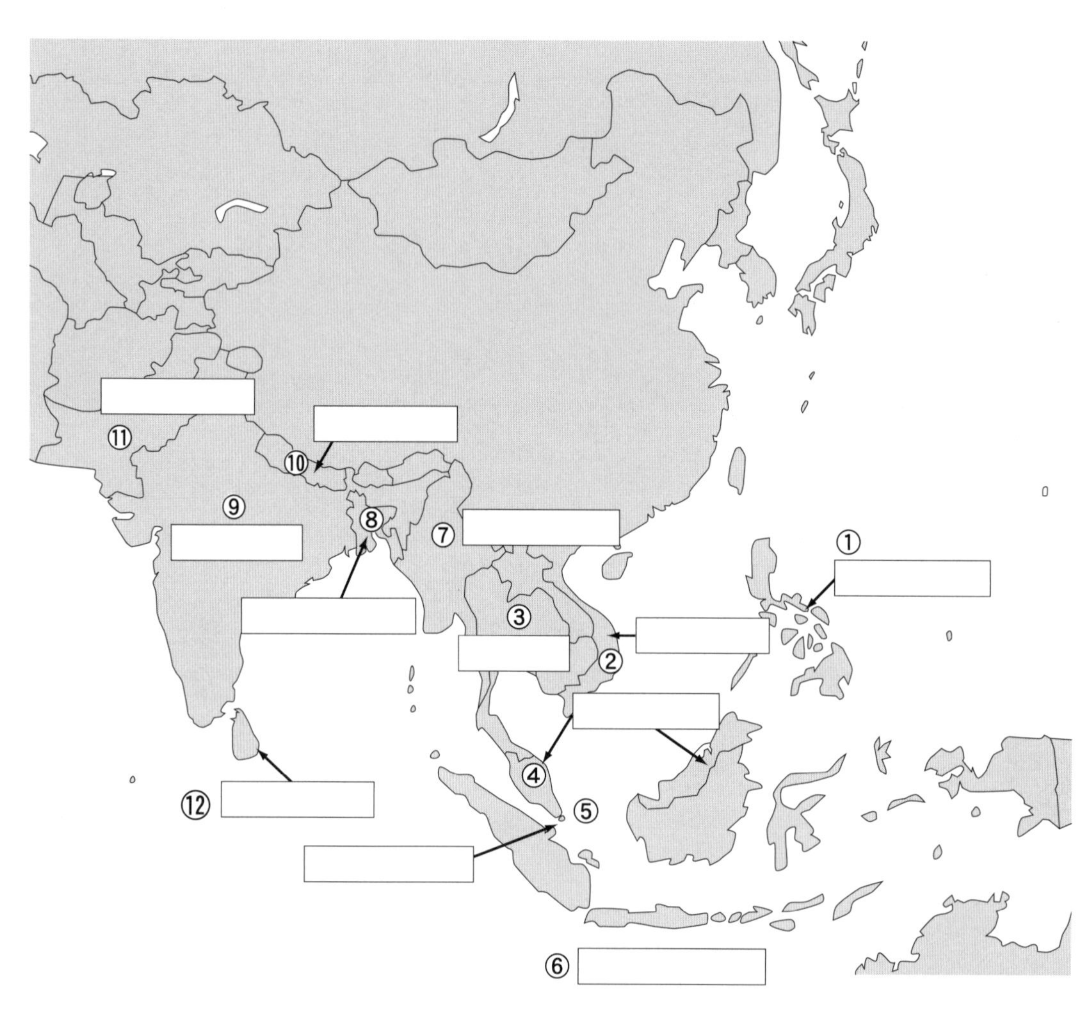

①Fi-ri-pi-n (Philippines)
②Be-to-na-mu (Vietnam)
③Ta-i (Thailand)
④Ma-rē-shi-a (Malaysia)
⑤Shi-n-ga-pō-ru (Singapore)
⑥I-n-do-ne-shi-a (Indonesia)
⑦Mya-n-mā (Myanmar)
⑧Ba-n-gu-ra-de-shu (Bangladesh)
⑨I-n-do (India)
⑩Ne-pā-ru (Nepal)
⑪Pa-ki-su-ta-n (Pakistan)
⑫Su-ri-ra-n-ka (Sri Lanka)

Summary Quiz (3)

Write the names of the countries in the boxes in katakana by referring to the names written in *Romaji* below.

①I-gi-ri-su	(United Kingdom)	②Fu-ra-n-su	(France)
③Do-i-tsu	(Germany)	④O-ra-n-da	(Netherlands)
⑤Pō-ra-n-do	(Poland)	⑥Che-ko	(Czech)
⑦Ō-su-to-ri-a	(Austria)	⑧Su-i-su	(Switzerland)
⑨I-ta-ri-a	(Italy)	⑩Su-pe-i-n	(Spain)
⑪Po-ru-to-ga-ru	(Portugal)	⑫No-ru-wē	(Norway)
⑬Su-wē-de-n	(Sweden)	⑭Fi-n-ra-n-do	(Finland)

26 Comprehensive Exercise

1. Reading Practice

26-1

Read the names of the meals and drinks from 1 to 20 in the menu below.

メニュー

おしょくじ

1	カレーライス	600
2	エビピラフ	700
3	ビーフシチュー（ライスまたはパン）	850
4	スパゲティーミートソース	650
5	バタートースト	250
6	ミックスサンドイッチ	550
7	ハンバーガー	350
8	ツナサラダ	300

おのみもの

9	コーヒー	400
10	カフェオレ	450
11	レモンティー	400
12	ミルクティー	450
13	オレンジジュース	550
14	コーラ	400
15	クリームソーダ	450
16	ビール	350

デザート

17	フルーツヨーグルト	450
18	バニラアイスクリーム	450
19	チョコレートパフェ	650
20	ケーキセット（ケーキ、コーヒー）	650

menyū (menu)
o-shokuji (meals)
1. karē raisu (curry and rice)
2. ebi pirafu (pilaf with shrimp)
3. biifu shichū [raisu matawa pan] (beef stew [rice or bread])
4. supagetii miito sōsu (spaghetti with meat sauce)
5. batā tōsuto (buttered toast)
6. mikkusu sandoitchi (mixed sandwich)
7. hanbāgā (hamburger)
8. tsuna sarada (tuna salad)

o-nomimono (drinks)
9. kōhii (coffee)
10. kafe o re (café au lait)
11. remon tii (tea with lemon)
12. miruku tii (tea with milk)
13. orenji jūsu (orange juice)
14. kōra (Coca-Cola)
15. kuriimu sōda (ice-cream soda)
16. biiru (beer)

dezāto (dessert)
17. furūtsu yōguruto (fruit yoghurt)
18. banira aisu kuriimu (vanilla ice cream)
19. chokorēto pafe (chocolate parfait)
20. kēki setto [kēki, kōhii] (cake set [cake, coffee])

2. Reading Practice

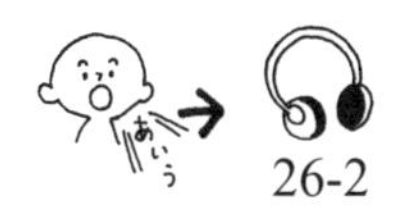

1） あした → たばこ → コート → とりにく → クラス → すずしい → インド → ドア

2） げんき → きそく → くるま → マッチ → ちかてつ → つくえ → エアメール

3. Listening and Writing Exercise

Listen to the CD and complete the words in the boxes. Note that the first letter of each word is the same as the last letter of the previous word.

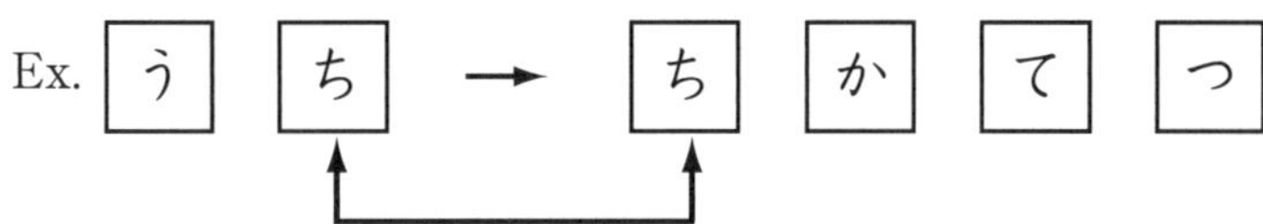

1）
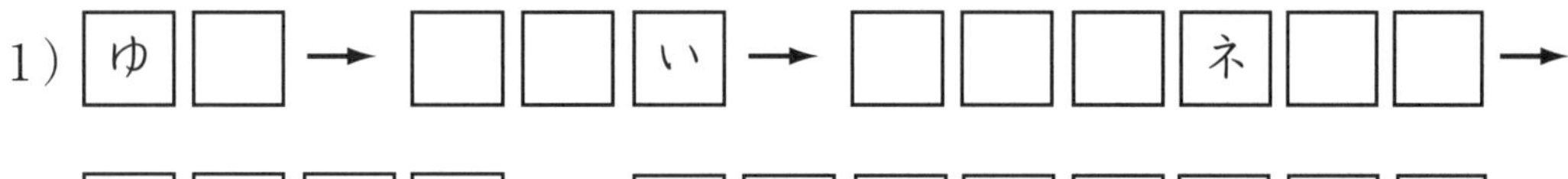

2）
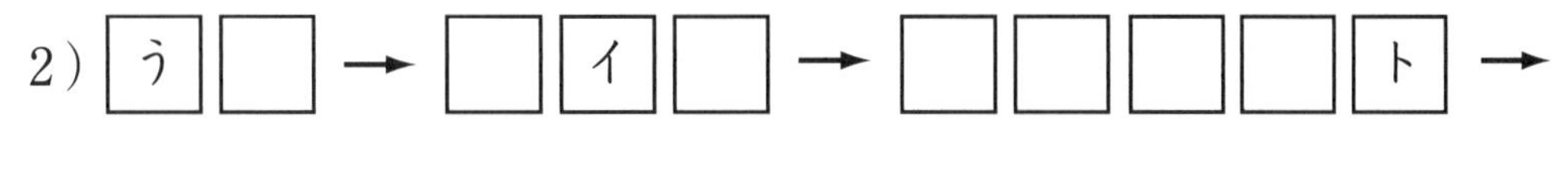

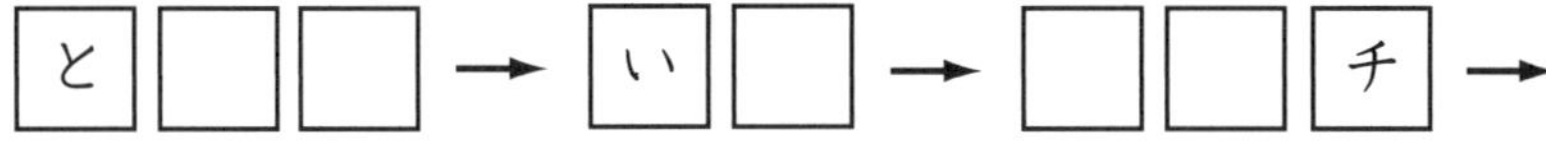

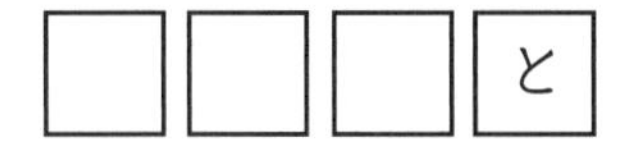

---

2. 1) tomorrow, tobacco, coat, chicken, class, cool, India, door

2) healthy, rule, vehicle, match, subway, desk, airmail

4. Reading Practice

26-4

Ex.

こんにちは。
わたしは　すずきです。

1）

わたしは　あさ
7（しち）じに　おきます。

2）

パンを　たべます。そして、
コーヒーを　のみます。

3）

8（はち）じに　かいしゃへ
いきます。

4）

9（く）じから　5（ご）じまで
はたらきます。

5）

それから、バスで
うちへ　かえります。

5. Listening and Writing Exercise

26-5

1）＿＿＿＿＿＿＿＿＿＿＿＿＿＿＿＿＿

2）＿＿＿＿＿＿＿＿＿＿＿＿＿＿＿＿＿＿＿＿＿＿＿＿＿＿

3）＿＿＿＿＿＿＿＿＿＿＿＿＿＿＿＿＿＿＿＿＿＿＿＿＿＿

4）＿＿＿＿＿＿＿＿＿＿＿＿＿＿＿＿＿＿＿＿＿＿＿＿＿＿

5）＿＿＿＿＿＿＿＿＿＿＿＿＿＿＿＿＿＿＿＿＿＿＿＿＿＿

---

4. Ex. Hello. My name is Suzuki.　1) I get up at 7 o'clock in the morning.
2) (I) eat bread and drink a cup of coffee.　3) (I) go to work at 8 o'clock.
4) (I) work from 9:00 to 5:00.　5) Then, (I) go back to my house by bus.

Hiragana Picture Cards

The combination of a hiragana letter with a drawing expressing the meaning of a Japanese word enables students who are learning hiragana for the first time to become readily familiar with those letters.

These cards are particulary useful for students who want to be able to read hiragana even if they do not need to write Japanese.

HOW TO USE THE CARDS

1. Confirm the pronunciation of the letter by doing the listening practice specified in the workbook. Then memorize the shapes of the letters as much as possible while looking at the picture cards. If you have not learned the word on the card yet, the translation cards for the words will give you the meaning.
2. After learning how to read the letters, separate the cards, shuffle them, and practice reading them.
3. When learning letters with similar shapes, comparing the differences in the drawings on the cards will help you effectively remember them (ex: 41. る vs 43. ろ).

1．あ
2．い
3．う
4．え
5．お
1
2
3
1．あ　ame: rain
2．い　ichi-ban: no. 1
3．う　ue: on, above
4．え　e: picture
5．お　ongaku: music

6. か kaban: bag
7. き kirimasu: cut
8. く kuchi: mouth
9. け kekkon: marriage
10. こ kōcha: black tea

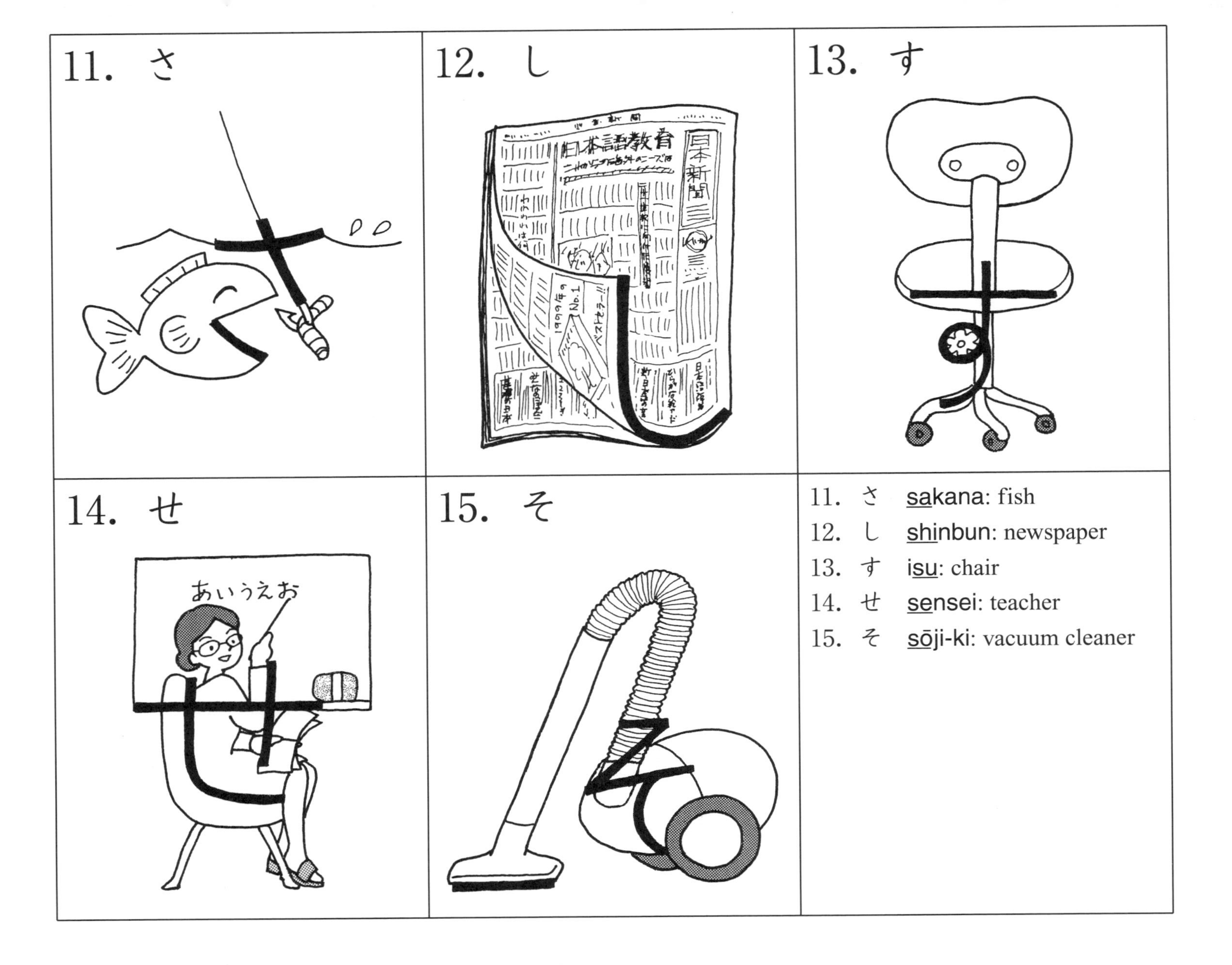

11. さ　sakana: fish
12. し　shinbun: newspaper
13. す　isu: chair
14. せ　sensei: teacher
15. そ　sōji-ki: vacuum cleaner

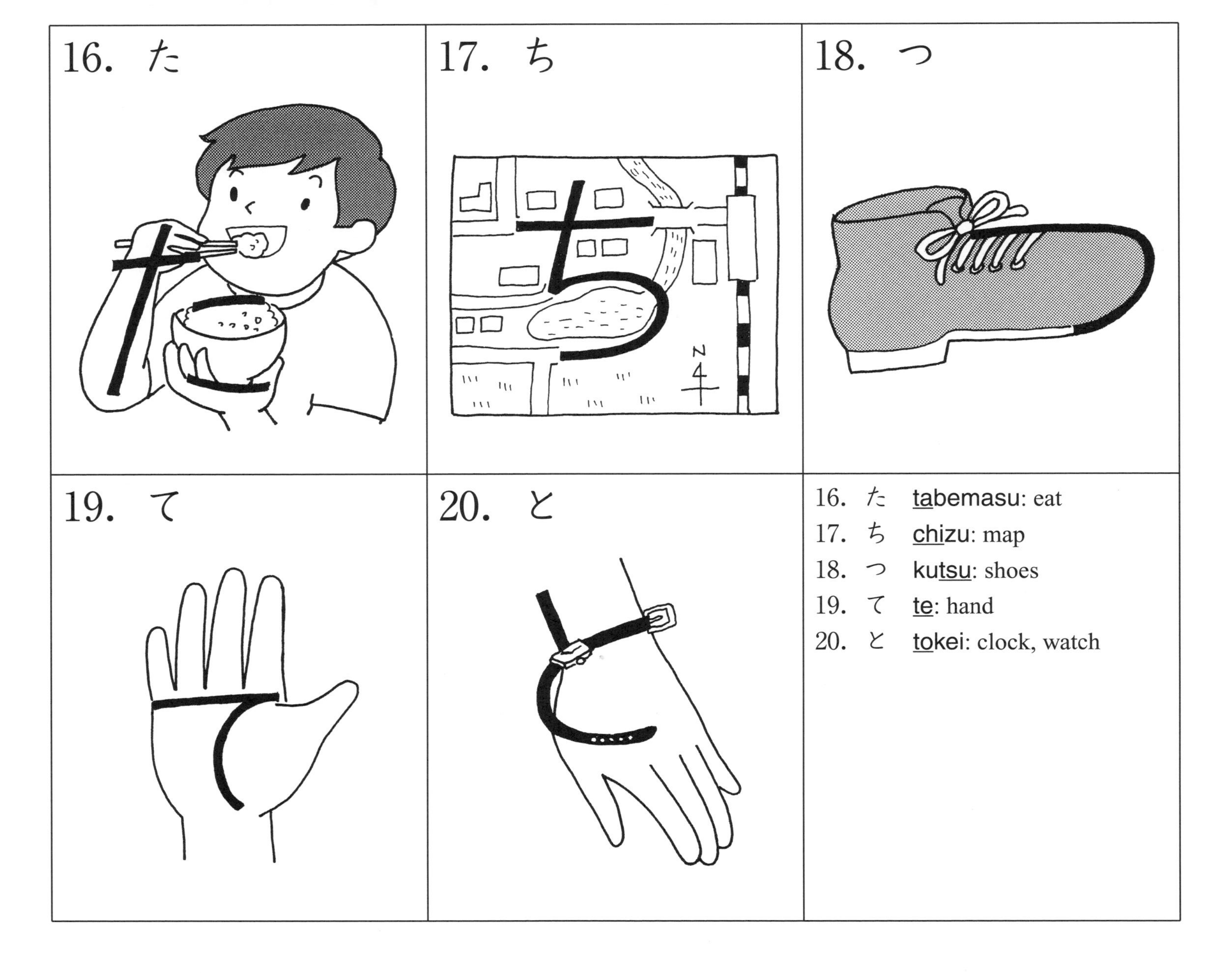
16. た
17. ち
N
18. つ
19. て
20. と
16. た tabemasu: eat
17. ち chizu: map
18. つ kutsu: shoes
19. て te: hand
20. と tokei: clock, watch

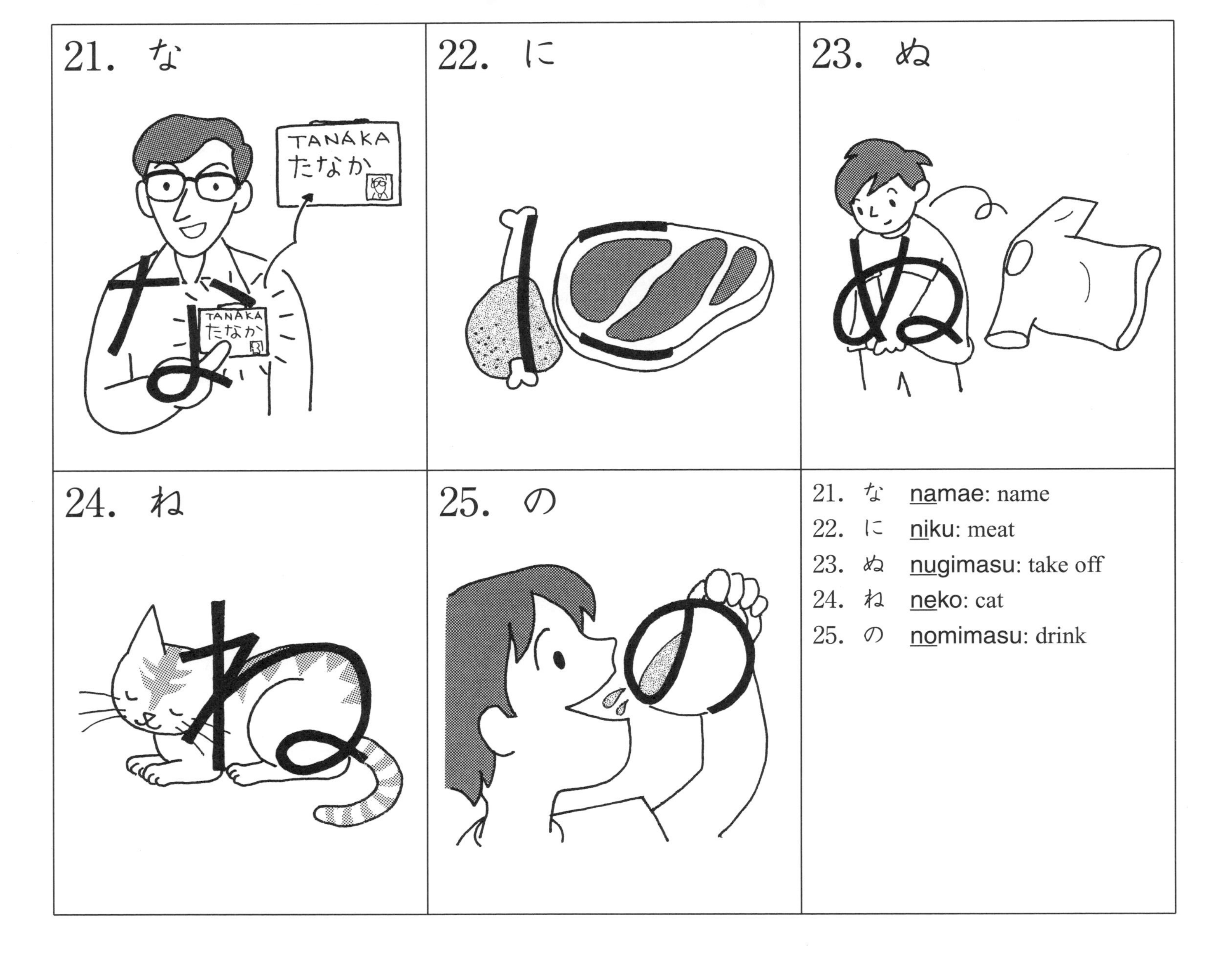

21. な
TANAKA
たなか
TANAKA
たなか
22. に
23. ぬ
24. ね
25. の
21. な namae: name
22. に niku: meat
23. ぬ nugimasu: take off
24. ね neko: cat
25. の nomimasu: drink

26. は
27. ひ
28. ふ
29. へ
30. ほ
26. は hana: flower
27. ひ hito: person
28. ふ Fujisan: Mt. Fuji
29. へ heya: room
30. ほ hon: book

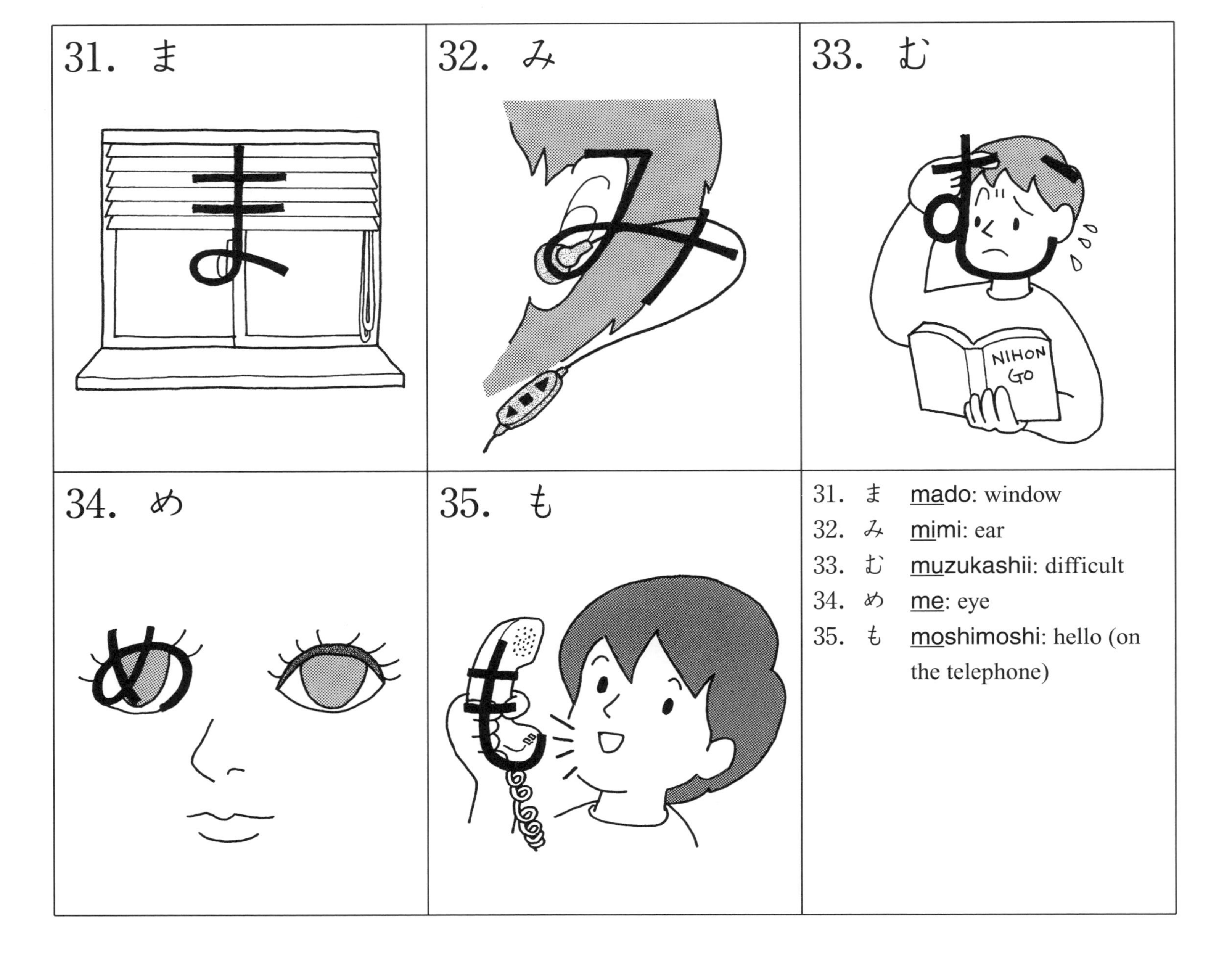

31. ま
32. み
33. む
NIHON GO
34. め
35. も
31. ま mado: window
32. み mimi: ear
33. む muzukashii: difficult
34. め me: eye
35. も moshimoshi: hello (on the telephone)

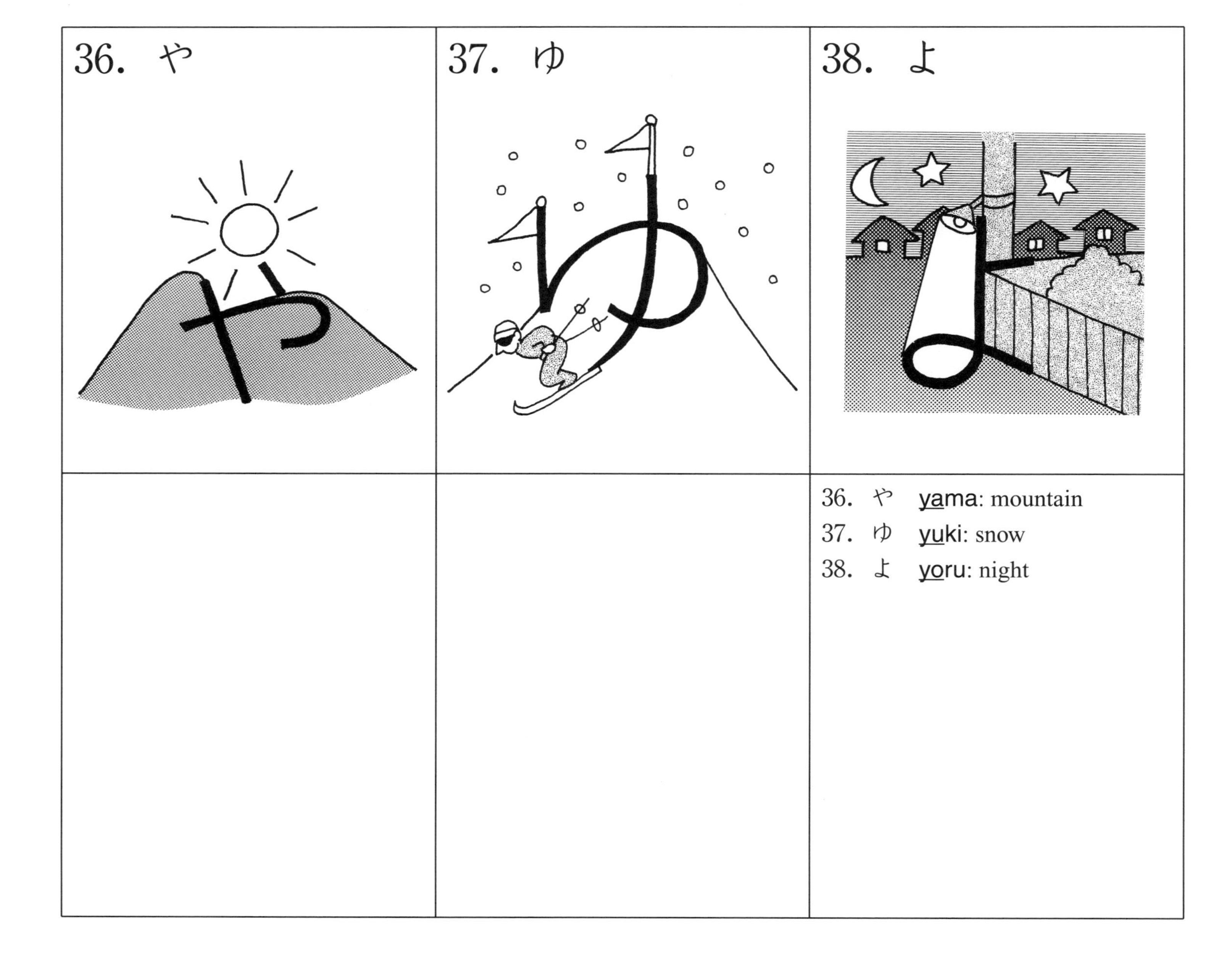

36. や　yama: mountain
37. ゆ　yuki: snow
38. よ　yoru: night

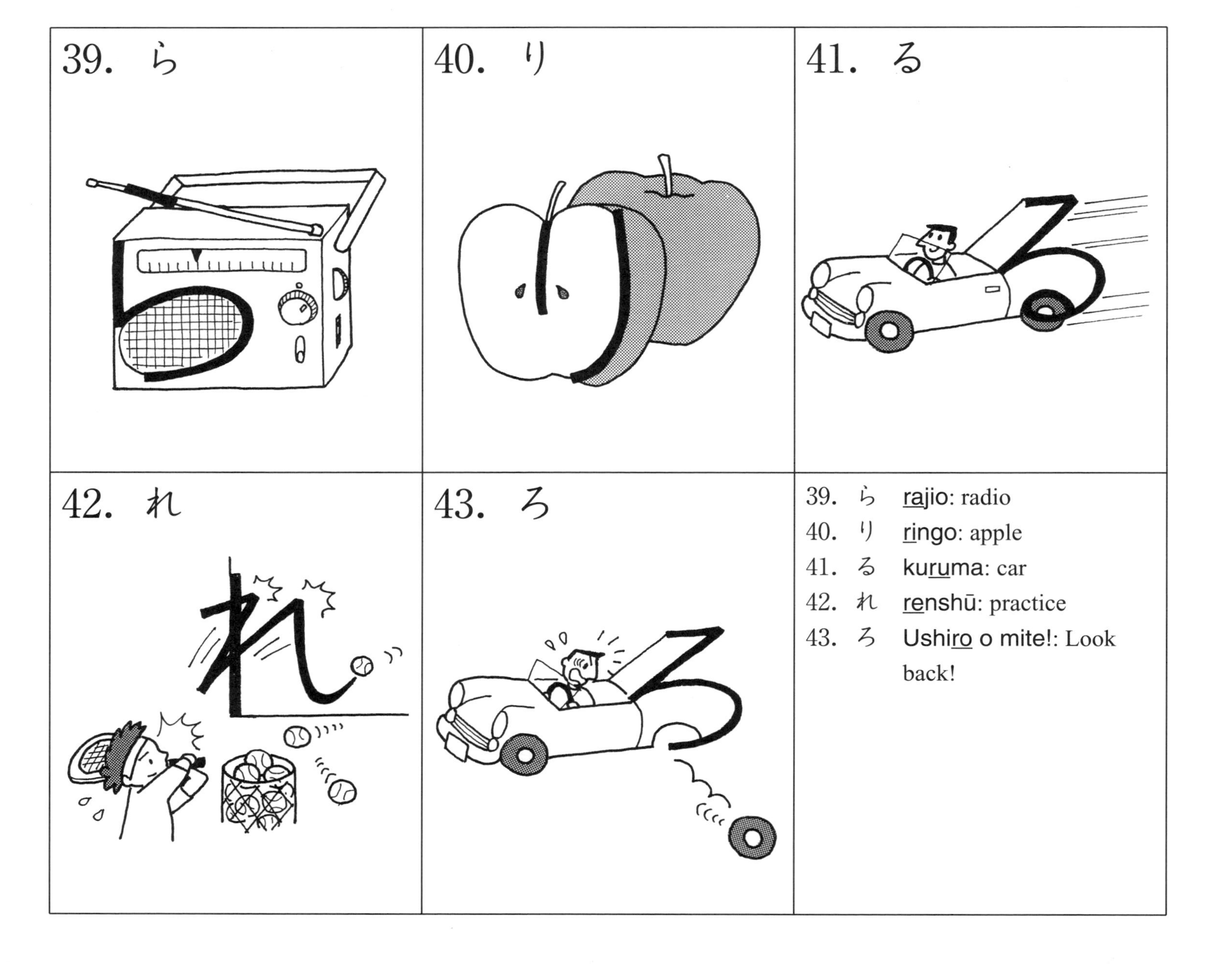

39. ら rajio: radio
40. り ringo: apple
41. る kuruma: car
42. れ renshū: practice
43. ろ Ushiro o mite!: Look back!

44. わ

45. を

46. ん

44. わ Wa!: Wow!

45. を tamago o tabemasu: eat an egg

46. ん nnn!: Ummm! (When leaning to the right, “h” will look like ん.)

イラスト
多羅日奈子

表紙デザイン
片岡　理

英語版
一人で学べる　ひらがな　かたかな

2000年6月25日　初版第1刷発行
2019年6月21日　第 19 刷 発 行

著作・編集　一般財団法人　海外産業人材育成協会（AOTS）
（旧）財団法人　海外技術者研修協会（AOTS）
発 行 者　藤嵜政子
発　　行　株式会社スリーエーネットワーク
〒102-0083　東京都千代田区麹町3丁目4番 トラスティ麹町ビル2F
電話　営業　03（5275）2722
　　　編集　03（5275）2725
https://www.3anet.co.jp/
印　　刷　日本印刷株式会社

ISBN978-4-88319-158-1 C0081
落丁・乱丁本はお取り替えいたします。

ANSWERS

p.3－3

1）

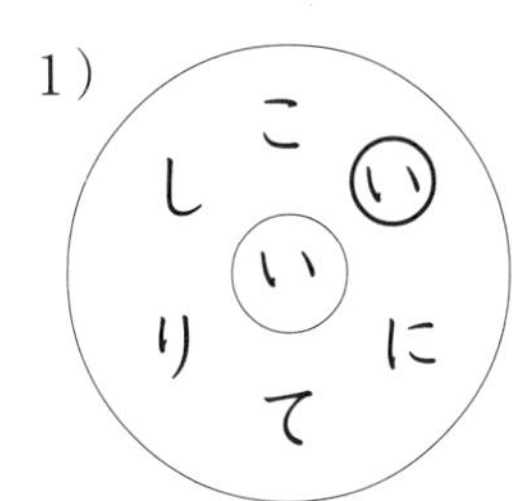

2）

ら
う
つ
う
や
え
ろ

3）

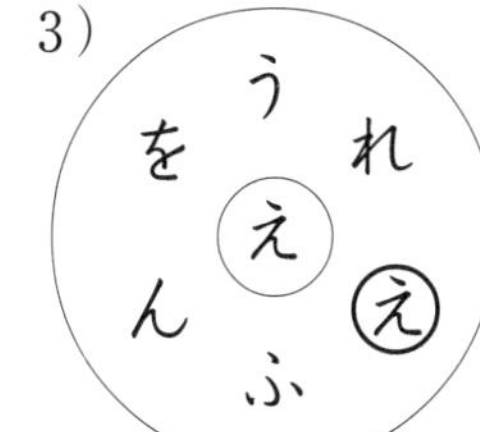

4）

あ
ゆ
め
お
お
の
わ

p.6－5

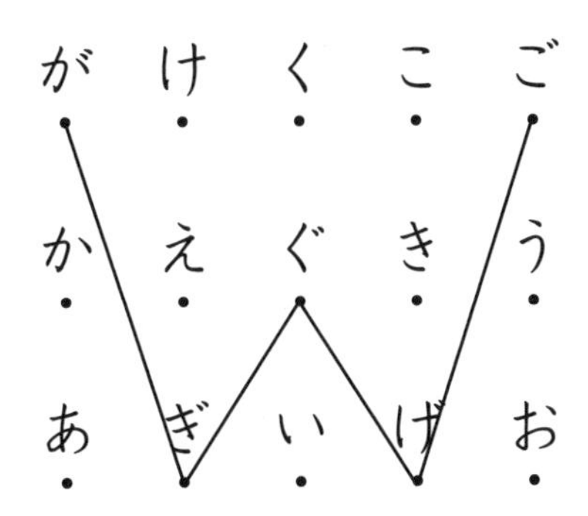

p.10－1

1） ue (up, above)　2） koe (voice)　3） kega (injury)　4） kagi (key)

5） aoi (blue)　6） gaikoku (foreign country)

p.10－2

1） ごご (afternoon)　2） かぎ (key)　3） えき (station)　4） かお (face)

5） きかい (machine)　6） いいえ (no)　7） がいこく (foreign country)

p.11－5

p.14－5

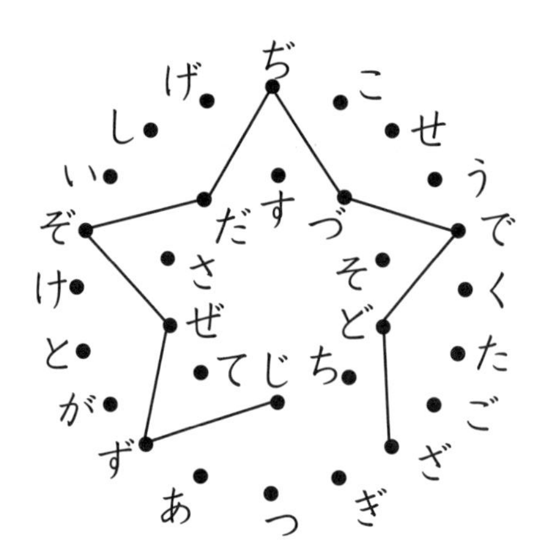

p.17－1

1） uso (lie)　2） ude (arm)　3） kutsu (shoes)　4） jiko (accident)

5） kaze (flu, cold)　6） shizuka (quiet)　7） chikatetsu (subway)

p.17－2

1） かさ (umbrella)　2） どこ (where)　3） せかい (world)　4） かぞく (family)

5） すこし (a little)　6） たいせつ (important)

7） おととい (the day before yesterday)

p.18－3

1） c　2） b　3） a　4） b　5） d

p.22－7

1）	ふかふか	：	**ぷかぷか**	2）	**ふかふか**	：	ぶかぶか
3）	ひくひく	：	**びくびく**	4）	ぺたぺた	：	**べたべた**
5）	**ぱたぱた**	：	ばたばた	6）	**ぽきぽき**	：	ぼきぼき

p.25－1

1） hana (flower)　2） inu (dog)　3） fune (ship)　4） nani (what)

5） boku (I; informal form of "*watashi*" used by men)　6） nodo (throat)

7） tabako (tobacco, cigarette)　8） koibito (girlfriend/boyfriend)

9） kabuki (Japanese classical drama)　10） pokapoka (warm)

p.25－2

1） なに (what)　2） ひと (person)　3） へた (be poor at)　4） ふね (ship)

5） たばこ (tobacco, cigarette)　6） ほそい (thin)　7） あぶない (dangerous)

p.26－5

や	**お**	**よ**	**ぐ**	さ	い	ま	ぬ
み	ゆ		お	ぐ	**さ**	**む**	**い**
め	ぬ	**と**	**も**	**だ**	**ち**	み	
さ	ち	お	よ	ゆ		て	あ
	お	ぐ	や	む	**や**	**ま**	
て	が	み	か	**あ**	**め**		ゆ
こ			よ	**ゆ**	**き**	だ	め

p.29－5

み	ろ	**ひ**	**だ**	**り**	わ	た	と
ち	**よ**	**る**	つ	ひ	**ど**	**れ**	ね
よ	ろ	め		ど	**わ**	**た**	**し**
わ	な	ま	え	ぬ	ど	わ	よ
り	と	れ	**い**	**く**	**ら**	の	れ

p.32－1

1）yama (mountain)　2）yoru (night)　3）dore (which one)
4）ame (rain)　5）yuki (snow)　6）musuko (son)
7）ikura (how much)　8）watashi (I)
9）mikan (mandarin orange)　10）tomodachi (friend)

p.32－2

1）みず (water)　2）ふゆ (winter)　3）ひる (day time, noon)
4）さむい (cold, chilly)　5）しろい (white)　6）なまえ (name)
7）ひだり (left [side])　8）りんご (apple)　9）のみもの (drink)
10）よみます (read)

p.33

1 く　2 へ　3 い　4 こ　5 う　6 ら
7 た　8 に　9 る　10 ろ　11 き　12 さ
13 す　14 む　15 は　16 ほ　17 ま　18 あ
19 め　20 ぬ　21 ね　22 れ　23 わ

p. 34

あ a	い i	う u	え e	お o
か ka	き ki	く ku	け ke	こ ko
さ sa	し shi	す su	せ se	そ so
た ta	ち chi	つ tsu	て te	と to
な na	に ni	ぬ nu	ね ne	の no
は ha	ひ hi	ふ fu	へ he	ほ ho
ま ma	み mi	む mu	め me	も mo
や ya		ゆ yu		よ yo
ら ra	り ri	る ru	れ re	ろ ro
わ wa				を o
ん n				

が ga	ぎ gi	ぐ gu	げ ge	ご go
ざ za	じ ji	ず zu	ぜ ze	ぞ zo
だ da	ぢ ji	づ zu	で de	ど do

ば ba	び bi	ぶ bu	べ be	ぼ bo
ぱ pa	ぴ pi	ぷ pu	ぺ pe	ぽ po

p. 35

1）ほん (book)　2）しんぶん (newspaper)　3）えんぴつ (pencil)
4）てがみ (letter)　5）かぎ (key)　6）かばん (bag)
7）たばこ (tobacco, cigarette)　8）はいざら (ashtray)
9）ちず (map)　10）でんわ (telephone)　11）くつ (shoes)
12）ふね (ship)　13）つくえ (desk)　14）いす (chair)
15）まど (window)　16）りんご (apple)　17）さかな (fish)
18）にく (meat)　19）やさい (vegetable)　20）たまご (egg)

p．38－2

1）ま：まあ　2）い：いい　3）ふ：ふう　4）ね：ねえ

5）と：とお　6）も：もう　7）ほし：ほしい

8）くろ：くろう　9）ゆめ：ゆうめい　10）こてい：こうてい

p．39－4

1．1）お|じ|い|さん　2）お|ば|あ|さん　3）お|と|う|さん

4）お|か|あ|さん　5）お|に|い|さん　6）お|ね|え|さん

7）い|も|う|と　8）お|と|う|と

p．39－4

2．1）ちいさい (small)　2）おいしい (delicious)　3）えいが (movie)

4）とおい (far)　5）きのう (yesterday)　6）ゆうめい (famous)

p．41－4

1）けっこん (marriage)　2）がっこう (school)

3）あさって (the day after tomorrow)　4）|ま|っ|て|　ください (Please wait.)

5）りんごが　|み|っ|つ|　あります (There are three apples.)

p．48－1

1）tokei (watch, clock)　2）ohayō (good morning)　3）zasshi (magazine)

4）asatte (the day after tomorrow)　5）ocha (tea)　6）kyō (today)

7）kaisha (company)　8）gyūnyū (milk)

p．48－2

1）みっつ (three)　2）きって (postage stamp)　3）ふうとう (envelope)

4）おおきい (big)　5）ゆっくり (slowly)　6）ちょっと (a little)

7）じしょ (dictionary)　8）ちゅうごく (China)

9）びょういん (hospital)　10）こうじょう (factory)

p．51－2

1）わたしは　がくせい　では　ありません。(I'm not a student.)

2）おとうとは　とうきょうへ　いきます。

(My younger brother will go to Tokyo.)

3）りんごを　みっつ　ください。(Please give me three apples.)

4）きょうは　やすみです。(Today is a holiday.)

5）にちようび　えいがを　みます。(I'll see a film on Sunday.)

6）せんしゅう　にほんへ　きました。(I came to Japan last week.)

p.53−3

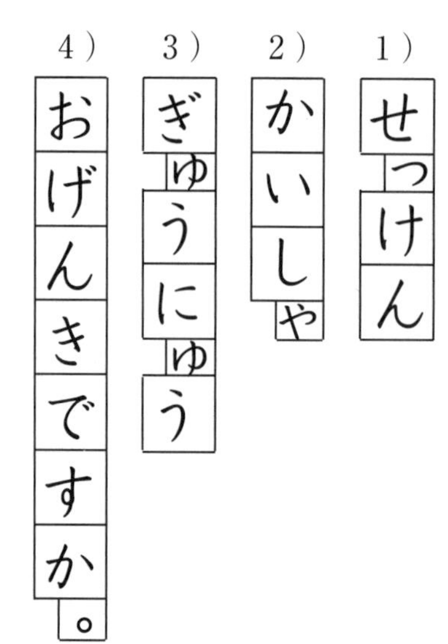

p.54

1）

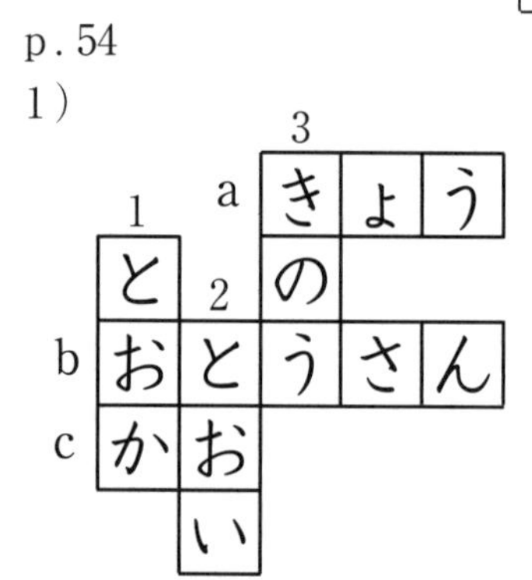

2）

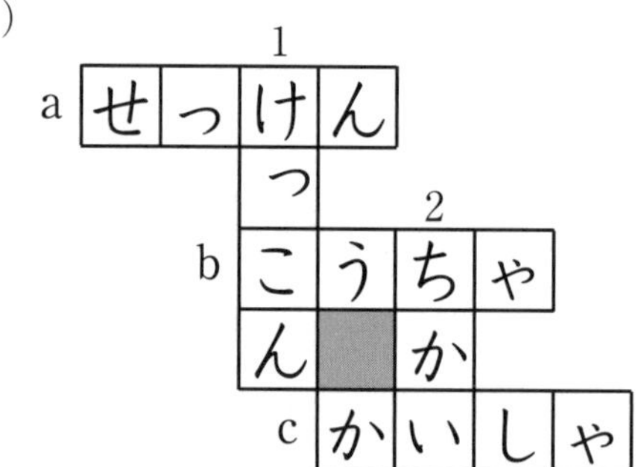

3）

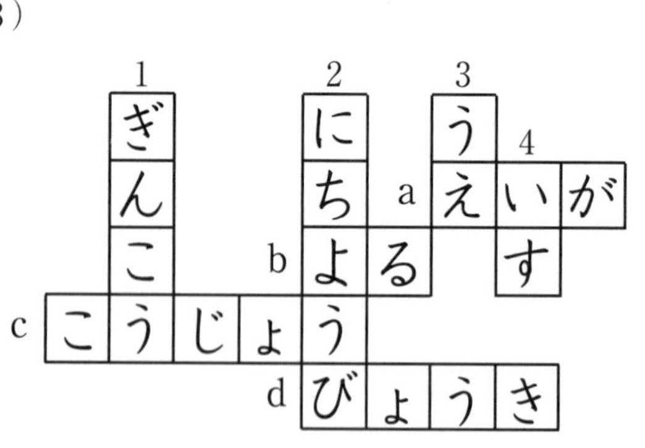

4）

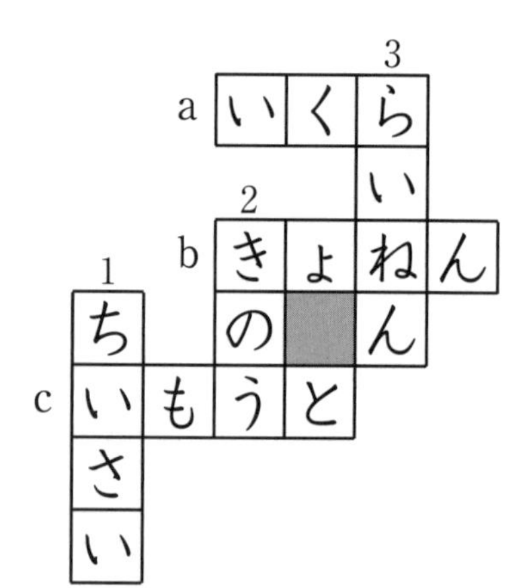

p．55－1

1）こうえん (park)　2）きっぷ (ticket)　3）がっこう (school)
4）おかあさん (mother)　5）おちゃ (tea)　6）りょこう (trip)
7）じゅうしょ (address)　8）きょうしつ (classroom)
9）にちようび (Sunday)
10）ちょっと　まって　ください (Please wait a minute.)

p．55－2

1）こんにちは。
(Hello.)
2）たなかさん、おげんきですか。
(How are you, Mr. Tanaka ?)
3）わたしは　らいしゅう　くにへ　かえります。
(I'm going back to my country next week.)
4）いろいろ　ありがとう　ございました。
(Thank you very much for everything.)
5）また　あいましょう。
(See you again.)

p．61－5

お	ん	あ	う	い	え
オ	ン	ア	ウ	イ	エ

p．64－5

こ	き	が	げ	ご	く	か	ぎ	け	ぐ
コ	キ	ガ	ゲ	ゴ	ク	カ	ギ	ケ	グ

p．67－5

ざ	そ	ぜ	さ	す	じ	せ	ぞ	し	ず
ザ	ソ	ゼ	サ	ス	ジ	セ	ゾ	シ	ズ

p．70－5

づ	ど	ぢ	と	た	で	ち	て	つ	だ
ヅ	ド	ヂ	ト	タ	デ	チ	テ	ツ	ダ

p. 72－1

1） doa (door)　2） dansu (dance)　3） saizu (size)　4） senchi (centimeter)

5） kōto (coat)　6） uisukii (whiskey)　7） enjin (engine)

p. 72－2

1）

い	と
イ	ト

2）

し	つ
シ	ツ

3）

そ	ん
ソ	ン

4）

く	た
ク	タ

5）

ち	て
チ	テ

p. 72－3

1） タイ (Thailand)　2） インド (India)　3） デザイン (design)　4） ギター (guitar)

5） タクシー (taxi)　6） センター (center)　7） セーター (sweater)

p. 74－5

の	に	ね	ぬ	な
ノ	ニ	ネ	ヌ	ナ

p. 78－5

ば	ぼ	ぱ	ぷ	ひ	ぶ	ぺ	は	ぴ	べ	ふ	ぽ	び	ほ
バ	ボ	パ	プ	ヒ	ブ	ペ	ハ	ピ	ベ	フ	ポ	ビ	ホ

p. 80－1

1） tenisu (tennis)　2） piano (piano)　3） banana (banana)　4） tēpu (tape)

5） enjinia (engineer)　6） beddo (bed)　7） suitchi (switch)　8） hotchikisu (stapler)

p. 80－2

1） ナイフ (knife)　2） ネクタイ (necktie)　3） ノート (notebook)

4） スポーツ (sport)　5） ビデオ (video)　6） ピンポン (table tennis)

7） サッカー (soccer)　8） ポケット (pocket)

p. 82－5

み	め	ま	も	む
ミ	メ	マ	モ	ム

p. 85－5

れ	ろ	る	ら	り
レ	ロ	ル	ラ	リ

p. 88－5

や	わ	よ	ゆ
ヤ	ワ	ヨ	ユ

p.90

1	シ	2	ツ	3	ア	4	マ	5	ナ	6	メ		
7	ス	8	ヌ	9	チ	10	テ	11	イ	12	ト		
13	セ	14	ヤ	15	コ	16	ユ	17	ク	18	ケ	19	ワ

p.91

あ ア	い イ	う ウ	え エ	お オ
か カ	き キ	く ク	け ケ	こ コ
さ サ	し シ	す ス	せ セ	そ ソ
た タ	ち チ	つ ツ	て テ	と ト
な ナ	に ニ	ぬ ヌ	ね ネ	の ノ
は ハ	ひ ヒ	ふ フ	へ ヘ	ほ ホ
ま マ	み ミ	む ム	め メ	も モ
や ヤ		ゆ ユ		よ ヨ
ら ラ	り リ	る ル	れ レ	ろ ロ
わ ワ				を ヲ
ん ン				

p.92

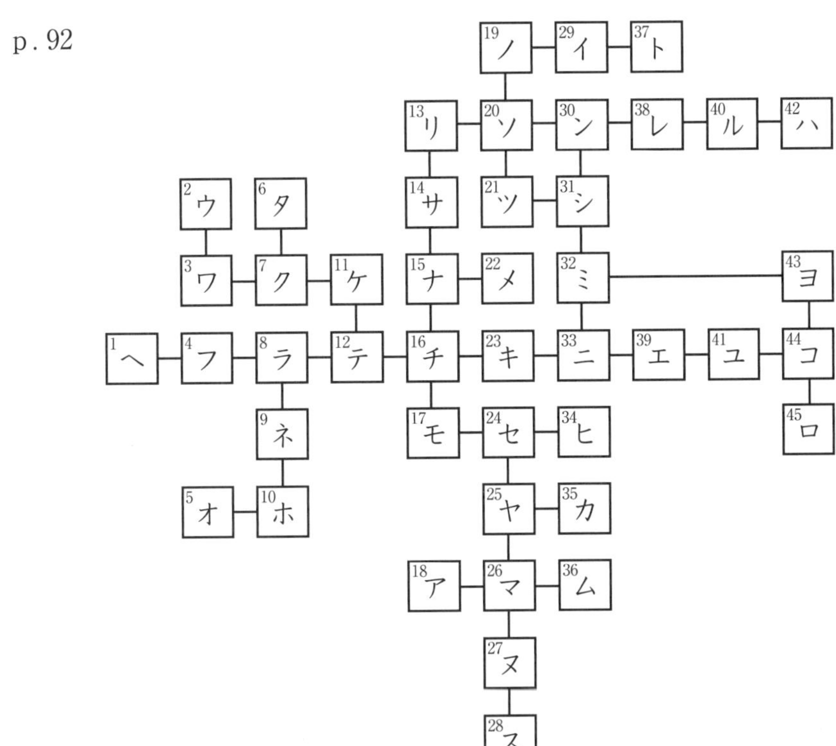

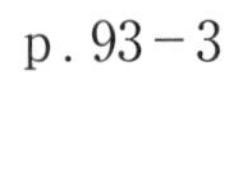
p. 93－3

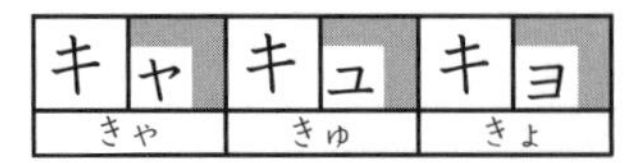

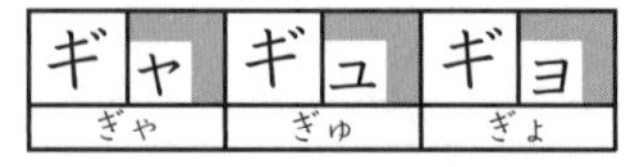

シャ	シュ	ショ
しゃ	しゅ	しょ

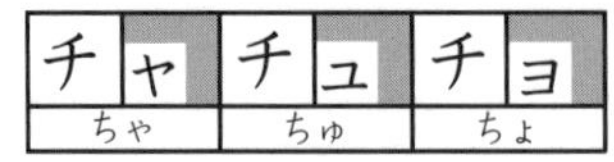

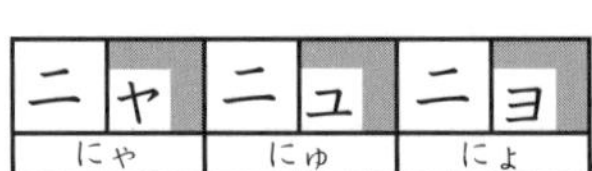

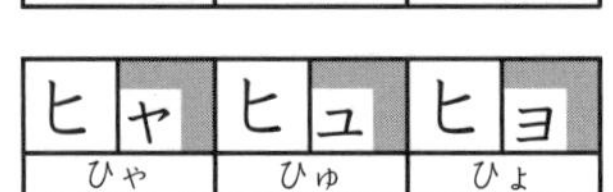

ビャ	ビュ	ビョ
びゃ	びゅ	びょ

ピャ	ピュ	ピョ
ぴゃ	ぴゅ	ぴょ

ミャ	ミュ	ミョ
みゃ	みゅ	みょ

リャ	リュ	リョ
りゃ	りゅ	りょ

p. 95－1

1） gomu (rubber)　2） miruku (milk)　3） rajikase (radio cassette tape recorder)

4） Marēshia (Malaysia)　5） shatsu (shirt)　6） konpyūtā (computer)

7） jogingu (jogging)

p. 95－2

1） ジュース (juice)　2） タイヤ (tyre)　3） タワー (tower)　4） メモ (memo)

5） メニュー (menu)　6） ロビー (lobby)

7） シャープペンシル (propelling pencil)

p. 99

1）

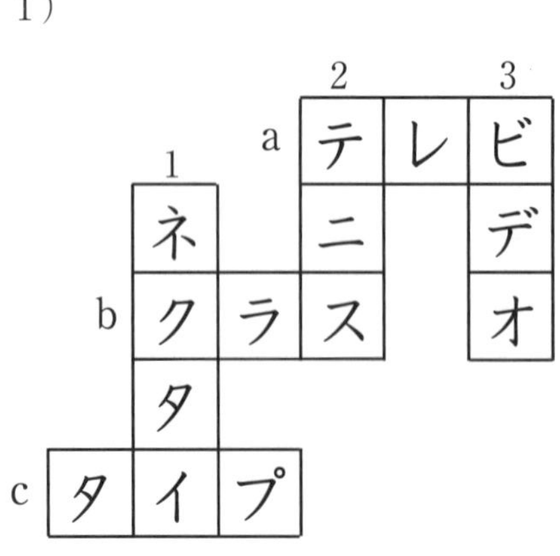

2）

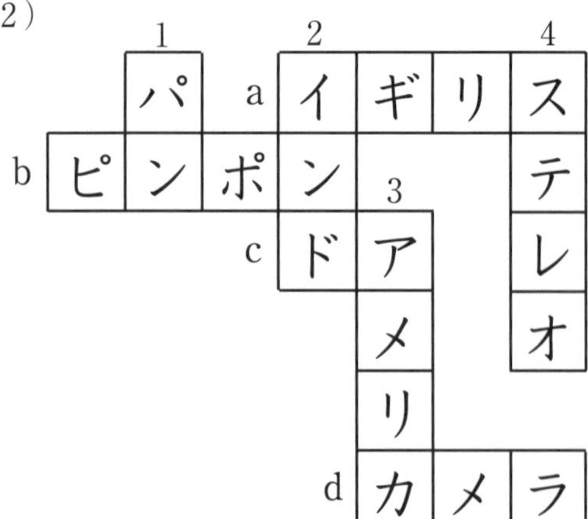

p. 100

1）テレビ (television)　2）トイレ (toilet)　3）ビル (building)
4）コーヒー (coffee)　5）ピアノ (piano)　6）ポスト (mail box)
7）シャワー (shower)　8）スーパー (supermarket)
9）ボールペン (ballpoint pen)　10）プレゼント (present, gift)
11）テープレコーダー (tape recorder)　12）ロボット (robot)
13）シャツ (shirt)　14）カメラ (camera)　15）パーティー (party)

p. 101

1. g　2. h　3. c　4. e　5. f　6. d　7. a
8. b　9. o　10. i　11. k　12. l　13. n　14. p
15. j

p. 102

①フィリピン　②ベトナム　③タイ　④マレーシア　⑤シンガポール
⑥インドネシア　⑦ミャンマー　⑧バングラデシュ　⑨インド
⑩ネパール　⑪パキスタン　⑫スリランカ

p. 103

①イギリス　②フランス　③ドイツ　④オランダ　⑤ポーランド
⑥チェコ　⑦オーストリア　⑧スイス　⑨イタリア　⑩スペイン
⑪ポルトガル　⑫ノルウェー　⑬スウェーデン　⑭フィンランド

p. 105－3

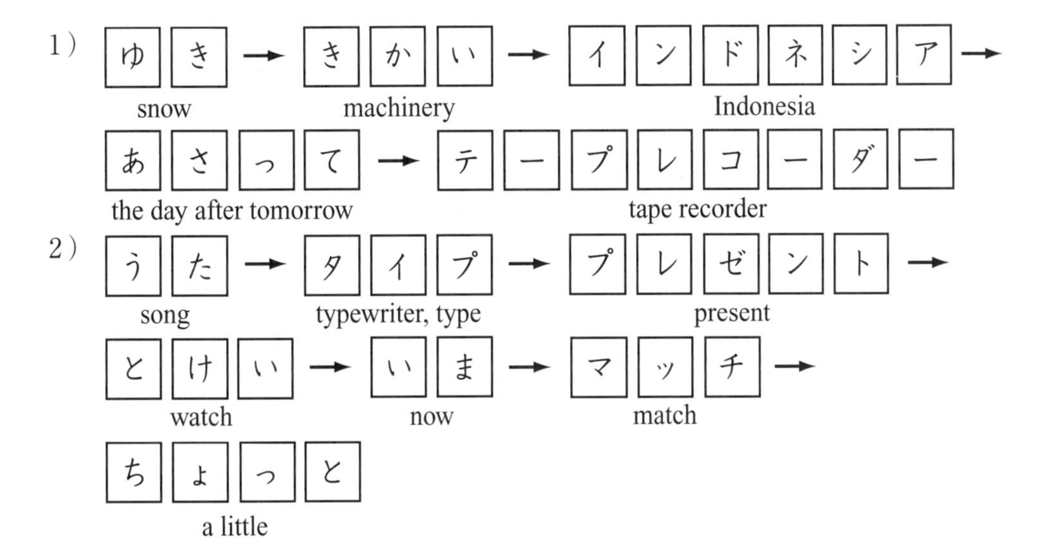

p．106－5

1）はじめまして。	How do you do?
2）わたしは　マレーシアの　リーです。	I am Lee from Malaysia.
3）きのう　にほんへ　きました。	(I) came to Japan yesterday.
4）せんもんは　コンピューターです。	My speciality is computers.
5）どうぞ　よろしく。	Nice to meet you.